LETTERS TO

ICELANDERS

EXPLORING THE

NORTHERN SOUL

BETTY JANE WYLIE

Macmillan Canada
Toronto

Canadian Cataloguing in Publication Data

Wylie, Betty Jane, 1931-
        Letters to Icelanders: exploring the northern soul

ISBN 0-7715-7635-8

1. Icelanders – Canada – Ethnic identity. 2. Icelandic Canadians
– Ethnic identity.* 3. Icelanders – United States – Ethnic identity.
4. Icelandic Americans – Ethnic identity. 5. Iceland – Civilization.
6. Wylie, Betty Jane, 1931-   . I. Title.

E49.2.I3W94 1999   305.83'961071   C99-930925-0

1 2 3 4 5   FP   03 02 01 00 99

Cover design by The Brookview Group, Gillian Tsintziras

We acknowledge the financial support of the Government of
Canada through the Book Publishing Industry Development
Program for our publishing activities.

This book is available at special discounts for bulk purchases
by your group or organization for sales promotions, premiums,
fundraising and seminars. For details, contact: CDG Books Canada
Inc., Special Sales Department, Suite 400, 99 Yorkville Avenue,
Toronto, ON M5R 3K5. Tel: 416-963-8830.

Macmillan Canada, CDG Books Canada Inc.
Toronto, Ontario, Canada

Printed in Canada

TABLE OF CONTENTS

PREFACE

When it comes to defining people's origins, most immigrants are tagged with a hyphen even as they are assimilated. Hyphens have only recently reached epidemic proportions, African-American seems lately to have led the pack. There's a descriptive tag so common to us north of the U.S. border that we don't even bother hyphenating it: French Canadian. Instead of being an Icelandic Canadian, I am labelled a Western Icelander, which is a descriptive phrase bestowed by Icelandic Icelanders, to indicate that (in their minds, anyway) those of us whose ancestors, one, two, three, even four generations back, came to North America from Iceland are just dropping by, having chosen to live in a different region somewhat to the west of where most of them still are.

I rather like the term Western Icelander; it gives me a foot in two worlds—a foot, but not a tongue. Like most later generations of Jóhanns-come-lately, I cannot speak Icelandic. That's the basic but not insurmountable gap between Western Icelanders and those who live in the "old country"—and I do mean old. While North America is getting set to celebrate the millennium, Iceland confidently prepares for its second, and counts on its offspring, wherever they are, to help. The small but enthusiastic enclaves of Western Icelanders scattered throughout North America do not share a common identity so much as an attitude, a realization that this facet that they have in common, this Nordic soul, is an enriching rather than a limiting one. We are defined by more than a hyphen.

Some born-and-bred patriots are saying, "My country, period, no antecedents necessary." Others are just picking up an enthusiasm for exotic food and a romantic landscape they want to explore—but not live in—and if they have to take on a new-to-them label, so be it.

No people have adjusted more completely to an adopted land than the Icelanders in North America. One historian has commented that the only places where these people retained their identity were ones previously uninhabited: Iceland and Greenland. Here in North America they're hidden, but mention Icelandic to anyone and you'll uncover an in-law, friend, colleague or acquaintance who is Icelandic, if not, indeed someone of direct descent. Both my married and my maiden name give no hint of my Icelandic heritage, but here I am. Icelanders seem to have been easily assimilated into the new nation, or did they infiltrate? They become an integral part of it almost by osmosis, entering into the essential life of the host, in this case, North America. This is certainly true in Canada. Have they lost their traditions? What happens to memory?

I think it remains, even in a fully assimilated Western Icelander, but in complicated layers. Call it déjà vu all over again. I have memories of sights never seen, lives never lived, even of a language never spoken, and a gut reaction to an astonishing, harsh, frozen, shining culture. I begin truly to believe in race memory. I begin to understand predilections that puzzled me and to acknowledge longings whose source I could not guess.

I went to Iceland in the summer of 1992 and again in the winter of 1995. I have seen more of it than my maternal grandparents did in their brief time in the land of their birth. In 1887 they left the country separately, my grandfather, Hans Pjetur Tergesen, from the north, near Akureyri, at age 24, and my grandmother, Sigriður Pálsdóttir, left Hofi in Hjaltadal, at 17. They met on the ship taking them to Canada, married in Winnipeg and moved first to Churchbridge, Saskatchewan, where they did not stay, then to Gimli on the shores of Lake Winnipeg to raise their family in the largest Icelandic settlement in North America. In Icelandic, *gimli* means "home of the gods," or, some say, "paradise." The Icelanders have always had a wry sense of humour.

Tergesen is actually a Danish name; my grandfather's grandfather moved from Iceland to Denmark (Danes did not use the patronymic by that time). Their daughter, my mother, Inga, was the only first-generation Tergesen to marry outside the Nordic bloodlines. Her husband, Jack McKenty, was an English Canadian (Irish, diluted by five generations in Canada where his Loyalist forbears fled to from upper New York during the American Revolution). When I was in Iceland the first time, I offered my history apologetically to relatives I had never met before, trying to explain my lack of the language. Sadly, in their attempts to adapt to a new country, immigrants tend to lose the ancestral language. By the time the third or fourth generation takes an interest, their language is difficult to retrieve without formal education, because mothers' knees are long gone. My mother's knees were not conducive to my learning Icelandic. In fact, she never encouraged me to learn it because she wanted to be able to gossip freely with her sisters and mother during the summers my family spent in Gimli when I was a child. However, my knowledge of Anglo-Saxon and Old Norse redeemed me somewhat in Iceland; it enabled me to understand some of what I heard and more of what I read.

Like most Icelanders, I turned out to be a student of language and a lover of words. As an undergraduate honours English student at the University of Manitoba, I studied Anglo-Saxon and translated *Beowulf*, the first epic poem ever set down in the English language (A.D. 1000, from 6th century oral narratives). Anglo-Saxon is much closer to Old Norse, hence closer linguistically to modern Icelandic than to modern English. Perhaps my reaction to Anglo-Saxon was the first hint of race memory. I loved the language so much that I returned to it for my Master's degree when I majored in 20th-century poetry and wrote my thesis on the work of the poet W.H. Auden. For my minor studies I explored not only Anglo-Saxon, but also Old Norse. I translated *Njal's Saga,* the first of the Icelandic sagas I was to read and love, though I have read very few, so far, of the estimated 700 in existence.

My most thrilling moment in Iceland occurred when I stood in front of a glass case in the archives museum in Reykjavik and read the first page of *Njal's Saga* on its original vellum sheet. The curator came over and we chatted a few minutes before he went back to his office. I realized after I had left the museum that we had been speaking in Icelandic!

W.H. Auden was very proud of his Scandinavian connections and used them as a catalyst for one of his books. In 1935, Auden's publishers sent him and the poet Louis MacNeice to Iceland to write a travel book. The two poets hired guides and Icelandic horses, slightly bigger than Shetland ponies, and camped out. Together they wrote a collection of casual, informative, frequently funny, fascinating essays, poems and reports, the whole entitled *Letters from Iceland,* dominated by Auden. The poet's famous poem "Letter to Lord Byron," in four cantos of 35 to 50 rhyme royal verses (rhyme scheme: ababbcc), first appeared in that book. Out of print and a collector's item when I was working on my degree, the book is back in circulation. In 1965, eight years before he died, Auden returned to Iceland and wrote a fresh introduction to the book but changed nothing else. A new edition of *Letters from Iceland* was published and is still in print. I bought a new copy in Iceland.

When I reread it after all those years, I decided to experiment not only with my impressions of this exotic island that is part of my heritage, but also with my exploration of what happened in the transplant. Icelanders have suffered a sea change into something rich and strange. Well, we began with something pretty rich and strange, too. I have written some letters of my own, not to Iceland but to Icelanders, including Western Icelanders, most of them related to me. One thing and another, I'm finding out who I am, at last, maybe. Tip of the iceberg.

ACKNOWLEDGEMENTS

I am indebted to two kinds of networks: human and electronic.

Never have I been so grateful to so many people for their help, information, generosity and encouragement as I have with this book. First, I want to thank Lorna and Terry Tergesen, to whom this book is dedicated, for their unfailing assistance and patience withal, no matter what questions I hurled at them.

After them, I must resort to alphabetical order because it would be hard to give any one person precedence over another. So my heartfelt gratitude goes out to Don Coles, Gail Einarsson-McLeery, Donald E. Gislason, Kristjana Gunnars, Guðrun Bjork Guðsteinsdóttir, Halfdan Helgason, Bill Holm, Katrina Koven, Helga Malis, Lillian Vilborg MacPherson, Daisy L. Neijmann, Njördur Njardvík, Sigríður Sigurðardóttir, Marjorie Swanson, Valgeir Valgarðursson, William Wolfe-Wylie and the good people at the Icelandic-Canadian newspaper, *Lögberg-Heimskringla*, and the Reykjavik newspaper, *Morgenblaðið*. As for the Internet, I have acknowledged URLS and sources in footnotes as I went along. Go ahead and explore! I do want to thank Susan Girvan, my editor. This was a difficult book for her to edit and she has retained her humour and good will admirably. So have I.

*To Lorna and Terry—
my friends and kin*

CANTO ONE
—LETTER TO W.H. AUDEN

Excuse me, Sir, the liberty I take
In thus addressing you. We never met,
Although I know you very well. Please make
Allowances for this bold fan, and let
Me tell you of the task I wish to set
Myself, with you beside me as my muse.
(You have no choice in this, you can't refuse.)

MacNeice and you explored in '35
By car and bus, especially by horse,
And wrote a book. And then in '65
You took another look, without remorse
Or second thoughts. It's selling well, of course,
Though dated now, a little antebellum.
Well, finally it's my turn for the vellum.

Unknown to you I was your protege,
Devoted to your words, in verse or prose.
I wrote my thesis at the apogee
Of your career. (My own small mark, God knows,
Is like a stone in water as it flows.)
Your thoughts were mine; I quoted all your views.
No wonder that I turn to you as muse.

Just three weeks after my M.A. I wed,
Flinging myself into eternal bliss.

All thoughts of you retreated from my head,
My lit'ry life deflected with a kiss—
No time to sit and think or reminisce.
Four kids, and I was reading Dr. Seuss
While poetry fell into sad disuse.

Now I propose a slightly different book,
At least a different focus than the one
You wrote. Letters to Icelanders—*a look*
At both worlds in the same way you have done,
With letters, notes, reports not all in fun
And even (this may cause your mind to totter)
A note about Vigdís Finnboggadóttir.

In short, some letters all about Iceland.
You're not the only one I want to write
And Iceland's not the only place I've scanned.
I've travelled some since I first saw the light
And many goodly realms have hit my sight,
Including Gimli where my forebears hied
When Hecla blew them out on the first tide.

I went to Gimli in the summertime
Though Winnipeg was where I lay my head.
The Gimli folk became my paradigm.
I ate ideas with my daily bread
As summer after summer I was fed
On Nordic lore and food and learned to care
For vínar terta, mysostur *and* skyr.

The insights travel brings to self and home
With room for tangents, notes and swift asides,
Comprise the subjects of your lengthy poem.
I'd like to do that, too, and add besides
Some comments of my own—a few broadsides

To do with Canada, my native land,
While weighing pros and cons about Iceland.

Letters to Icelanders *gives me scope —*
A trip in time as well as space,
Plus scenery and food. Just give me rope
And I will hang, or skip, but stay one pace
Ahead. It's not a contest or a race:
I will not write as much as you because
Attention span is shorter than it was.

So this, my opening salvo has to stop
With humbly begging everybody's pardon.
From you, Sir, first, for daring thus to drop
Your name. I beg you not your heart to harden.
We both know poetry's a public garden
With fountains and a pool where I can wish
To catch a rainbow of Icelandic fish.

—BJW

CHAPTER ONE

KINSHIP
—LETTER TO MY FRIEND
WHO HAS AN ICELANDIC *AMMA*

DEAR KATRINA:

I'm writing you, my friend, because we each have an Icelandic *amma*. Like me, and most Western Icelanders two and three generations removed from Iceland, you don't speak Icelandic so you'll empathize with what I have to say. This is what happens when people pull up their roots and transplant themselves: subsequent generations are hybrid, both more and less than they might have been if their roots had stayed in one place. And yet the through line! The goodwill! The deep, essential understanding! The kinship!

My chief memory now of my first visit to Iceland was of attempting to communicate with a newly discovered first cousin, once removed, Halldóra Sigfúsdóttir. I remember the laughter. Halldóra giggled at me as I attempted to babble my way through a conversation with the aid of an English/Icelandic dictionary and a lot of body language. We laughed together as I cut through a thicket of idiom. Her daughter Herborg (nickname, Hebba) eased our struggles when she came to visit and acted as translator. She speaks English quite well, like most Europeans of her generation. The Icelanders I met speak or get along in five or six languages, including, always, English. It makes a Western Icelander feel very humble, especially a Canadian one who is scarcely intelligible in French, which is supposed to be Canada's other official tongue.

I felt muted as I immersed myself in a country and culture that was so familiar and yet so frustratingly foreign. All the words, signs, ads, speech, songs and sounds that flow past are in another language. It was as if I had been deprived of my senses or had become invisible. I walked through the streets reacting, thinking, responding internally to the stimuli around me but unable to express what I was feeling. I smiled and frowned and nodded vigorously, and could feel my face congealing from using my facial muscles while trying so hard to communicate what I couldn't speak.

This is what happens when one is a stranger in a strange land: it is pointless to have any stray thoughts, because they cannot be expressed. People had enough trouble understanding me when I simply wanted a drink or needed to put my feet up. How could they possibly follow when I took a flying excursion into an idea? People who manage to write creatively in a language other than their native one are awesome.[1]

Bear with me, Katrina, and brace yourself to be continually in awe when you take your first trip back to a country you have never seen but never left. Your reactions will not be programmed just because I tell you what I learned. Of course, you are free to react as you please. But I think you will respond as I did to the instant, unexpected hospitality that I received. The reason for it, of course, was that I was *fjölskylda*—family.

When Halldóra took me in as her guest, she acknowledged me as family without question, and assumed also without question that I should stay with her on my first visit to Iceland. So after my two-week Ring trip around the island I spent the last week with her in a beautiful apartment in a new complex within walking distance of

---

1 The literary giants Joseph Conrad and Vladimir Nabokov spring to mind, but I can think of other writers less well known who have leapt the language barrier.

Kringlan shopping mall—unique there, but recognizable to anyone familiar with the malls of North America. The view from her vast picture windows was more foreign: the low mountains to the east of Reykjavik.

The first question we had to answer was exactly what our relationship was. As near as we could figure, listening to Hebba, as she worked it out with some books she dragged over to show me, and translate, was that Halldóra's mother was my grandfather's (half) sister, which makes me Halldóra's first cousin once removed,[2] and a half-step away—very close kin for Icelanders. At that point I had no idea of the Icelandic obsession with genealogy. Nor had I any idea that my grandfather had a sister (a half-sister) left behind in Iceland when he emigrated to Canada.

I was wined and dined by Hebba, who filled in as my translator, chauffeur and friend, and her husband Hreggviður; by Halldór, Halldóra's son, and his wife, Margrét, and taken sightseeing by Halldór's grown daughter, Kristín Valla, visiting from England along with her two children, whose names, Tómi and Katje (Tómas and Katryn), belied their Bristol accents—cousins all. They spoke English to me. Halldóra, being the older generation, spoke it the least. The others had all travelled or studied abroad and were fluent in English, also the other Scandinavian languages (except Finnish, which is not Nordic), as well as very passable German and a smattering of French and Italian.

If I hadn't had that taste of Anglo-Saxon and Old Norse at university, and listened to my grandparents and aunts and uncles gossip over my head when I was a child, I would have been totally lost. As it was, the familiar sounds flowed over me and I understood more than I could speak; that, of course, is how a child learns to speak her native tongue.

---

2 My mother and Halldóra were first cousins; as my mother's daughter, I am a first cousin, once removed.

Although Icelandic is reputedly one of the most difficult of modern languages because it still declines and conjugates, I like to think that I could pick up passable Icelandic if I lived in the country for six months. I'd like to try it.

In the American writer Kurt Vonnegut's book *Slapstick*, the last president of the United States wins on the ticket "Lonesome No More." He carries out his election promise by assigning every citizen a family, chosen at random with the help of a computer, using the names of familiar flora and fauna to group them together. Thus, all the people assigned a Daffodil clan are arbitrarily related; Lilies are another clan, and so on. Not only do these computer-generated relatives enjoy a sense of kinship and belonging, they believe that they have a lot in common with their Daffodil or Lily, or whatever, family members. Perhaps the same kind of kinship and longing for belonging links Icelanders and, by close complement, Western Icelanders. The Jews have a word for it in Yiddish: *landsmann*, meaning someone from the same land or place, countryman. So with Icelanders: we are all kin because we come from the same land, a little more than kin and so much more than kind—overwhelmingly kind and generous, in fact.

So there we were, strangers related by blood—quite thick in northern climes—smiling and nodding though unable to say much. I had begun an odyssey back in time, to a land of déjà vu, full of wonder. I think Halldóra took it more for granted than I did, that I, no longer a young woman, a widow like herself, with grown children and grandchildren of my own, should live with her for a week and try to patch together a fabric of family and memories of things that never happened or didn't exist except in the imagination. On rereading my diary from that first trip to Iceland, I find, tucked in amongst the appreciation of the scenery, a constant theme, in fact, two nagging, repetitive questions: Who am I? What am I doing here?

I returned to Iceland four years later to find out—at least, to find out more. I wanted to see what the country looked like in the dark, and to test a theory I had about the sagas. This time I travelled with my cousins: my first cousin, Terry Tergesen (his father and my mother were brother and sister) and his wife, Lorna, who was a Stefanson. Both of them are more like a brother and sister to me. Lorna is fluent in Icelandic, Terry less so, but comfortable; I'm still speechless.

The four years had wrought a significant change in Halldóra, no longer able to accommodate a guest, and too easily tired and confused. The goodwill still burned brightly, however, as bright as all the Christmas candles, lamps and electric garlands in the streets, and illuminated crosses on every grave in all the cemeteries across the land. There's no doubt we were celebrating light. Also shedding it.

I had arrived with questions that I hoped to have answered, the ones I asked the first time, and some new ones. I found a note in my diary from the second trip that expresses the bane of most travellers: "Wherever I go, I take me with me." Who is that person I'm travelling with? And how much does where I am matter—or even where I've been?

I had never seriously taken to heart the poignant feelings of immigrants who change their skies, especially in earlier centuries than ours when there was little likelihood of ever seeing their families or their homeland again. *Goodbye* meant God be wi'ye till we meet again—on the other side of life. They say *Vertu sæll,*[3] in Icelandic, meaning, *Go in health*.

For my part, assailed by memories of my summers in Gimli, I was overcome by a kind of double vision. I found myself looking at Halldóra as if she were my *amma*, my

---

3 When greeting a male.

grandmother Sigga, though in fact Amma was younger than Halldóra when she died at the age of 76, and I much older than the 17-year-old student who was just getting to know her when she died. You, Katrina, having taken the time to learn your *amma*'s story, and being more mature than I was, will not have that aching feeling of loss, the regret of not knowing. As it was, the lilt of Halldóra's language comforted me and made me feel safe, though I didn't understand the words. The food, though not quite the same as it was in Gimli, and tasting far better than I remembered it, also filled me with sweet satisfaction. Many of those tastes were acquired slowly by my Canadian palate; once acquired, they became addictive. (I go to a Thorrablót[4] in Toronto every year now in order to get my fill of *rulla pylsa*.)

Of course, my memories are old. The Gimli of my childhood fades into a 60-year-old past, another era, and today's Iceland swings vibrantly at the end of this century and millennium. In fact, Reykjavik has been named the cultural capital of Europe for the year 2000 as it faces its second millennium. The future is up for grabs. How do you say that in Icelandic?

I have to reconcile Past and Present, Here and There, and bring them together until they meld into a single time-space continuum—Now. If I can do this, I'll be well on my way to finding out who I am and where I'm at. I guess that's why I'm writing this book. I think it's probably the same reason you, Katrina, have written a book about your *amma*, and the reason that many of us, if we're introspective at all, embark on this search for family and meaning.

Your *amma* was born in Canada, grew up and went to school here. My *amma* was born in Iceland and left when

---

4 An Icelandic pig-out, aka a midwinter celebration. The first one in Canada took place in Winnipeg on January 25, 1884.

she was 17. She has been in my thoughts ever since I became aware of the Emigration Museum in Hofsos. What courage it must have taken for her not only to cross the ocean to a strange new world but also to trust her life to that young man she met on the trip! If it hadn't been for those two events, I wouldn't be here writing this.

I was 17 when she died, barely getting to know her as a person, and not even aware that at that age, she had already made the decision to leave her homeland and was on her way to a new world and a new life. I had long known her good cooking and her lethal way with gin rummy, which she taught me to play, but that was all I knew. Hers was the first funeral that left me with lasting memories, which I have used since at different times in different ways in my writing. I remember the private funeral service held in the house before we went to the church and my amazing ability to understand what the minister was saying in Icelandic because that was the year I had begun to study Anglo-Saxon. I remember Afi (I called him Grampa in those days) gazing at her in the open casket and saying in wonder how lovely she looked, just like the young girl he had married. I remember the church bells ringing after the service and the extra thunk after each note as the stressed metal of the frozen bells protested in the air. And I remember Afi turning his chair in the kitchen to face the window in the direction of the cemetery, though it was too far away for him to see it, because that's where she was. Between the two of them, they taught me a lot about family and love, lessons you have learned, too, Katrina.

Of course, I'm still learning. Old as I am now, just eight years short of the age of my *amma* at her death, I'm only now beginning to focus on these things, realizing who I am, where I came from, and perhaps, in time, what I'm doing here and where I'm going. This wonder and perpetual sense of discovery is not unique to the families of immigrants. It's shared by anyone who has been jarred enough out of an unquestioning acceptance of life's lot. We're all travellers on a path to somewhere. That's such a banal truth it seems hardly worth mentioning, except that each generation must discover it anew. With the intolerant wisdom of my age, I question whether my children have discovered it.

Families seem to alternate from generation to generation between being stable and stationary to being adventurous and uprooted. My *amma* and *afi* left their home country for another land; my English grandmother's parents left civilized Ontario for a more brazen atmosphere in Winnipeg. My grandfather Donald's Loyalist ancestors left the rebellious (1776) colonies for Canada; that made him four, my father five and me six generations Canadian on my father's side. My parents and their siblings pretty well stayed where they were. My husband's parents left Scotland, married in Winnipeg and raised their family there: those children and their offspring are now scattered in Ontario. Of my mother-in-law's many siblings, none remain. In fact, from that large family on both sides, there's no one left in Canada other than those Ontario nephews/cousins, and of course, me, plus three of my children and four of my grandchildren. (My daughter Kate and her family are in Boston.)

The Icelandic side of the family has been more effective in maintaining the line. The best evidence of that can be seen in the general store Afi opened in 1899. It remains a thriving concern, with a fourth generation of the family— Stefan Tergesen, my first cousin once removed, that is, Afi's great-grandson—running it. It's the only general store in Canada with that distinction now that Eaton's is managed by outsiders.

The question I want to ask is, when families uproot, what happens to memory: family memory, race memory, story and history, in short, to knowledge of self? Most nomadic people notoriously travel light. Do they have enough room for the baggage of tradition? I guess they do if they're Western Icelanders (or Mormons) who are enthusiastic to the point of fanaticism on the subject of family roots and heritage. They get it from the old country, where anything to do with genealogy—histories, lists, records, bloodlines—is ardently pursued. Then, too, they have a distinct advantage because their heritage is portable: the stories exist in the minds and hearts of the people.

Of course, this pursuit of family is easier in a country of 270,000, where most people are related in some way or other, and where everyone is known by the first name. I guess you know, Katrina, that everyone in Iceland is named, according to gender, after the father (thus, a boy is Jónsson, and a girl is Jónsdóttir), which makes it easier to know who's who. The Icelandic phone book lists each half of a married couple separately: Inga Jónsdóttir and Petur Stefánsson. Recently the law has been changed to allow children to take their mother's name as, Guðrun Ingudóttir instead of Guðrun Petursdóttir. This allowance for the matronymic takes into account chidren who have been born out of wedlock and raised by their mother with no father in sight, giving them a name they can identify with—their mother's daughter or son and not a missing man's child. As far as I can tell, there has never been a stigma attached to such children and their births are a common occurrence. The population of Iceland is so small, every new little soul is welcome. Couples who intend to marry might have two or three children before they can afford to wed.

The name rule was bent to accommodate the few foreigners who arrived in Iceland. In 1979 the country welcomed Vietnamese refugees when the boat people were seeking new homes. At first the laws required newcomers to take Icelandic names. Later, realizing how important a person's name is and how closely it is linked to one's identity, the government allowed foreigners to retain their foreign names as surnames; their first-born sons could also bear that name. However, subsequent sons and daughters are named after their father's first name, with *son* or *dóttir* added. These new people are gradually doing some intermarrying with Icelanders and changing the inbred homogeneity of Iceland, but not much. The "foreign" element in Iceland amounts to about one percent of the population.

Of course, the surnames locked in when the settlers arrived in Canada, and they lost their first link with the home-country's tradition. From then on, Western Icelanders used the name of the first male immigrant in the family: Jónasson or Magnusson or Thorlaksson or whatever, and in most cases eventually dropping the double *s*. My *amma* was Pálsdóttir but became Mrs. Tergesen and her children were Tergesens and not Pjeturssons or Pjetursdóttirs. Of course, Amma gave her children Icelandic names just as other Western Icelanders who married within the familial system passed on traditional names to their children, though they chose names more immediately recognizable and acceptable by English standards, and spelled them differently. Only later in life, in the last 10 years or so, have my cousin Margaret and my aunt Laura become Margrét and Lára, respectively, but those were easy names. When I went to Iceland I encountered some of the more esoteric ones that didn't cross the ocean, names like those of my cousins, Halldóra and Herborg, and Hebba's husband, Hreggviður, and here's a lovely one—Sesselyja. As for my *amma*, I never could pronounce her name when I was a child: Sigríður. Everyone called her Sigga for short.

Do you know, Katrina, there is actually a book in Iceland, quite recently published, which lists all the first names in the country? Not only that, it also gives the number of people bearing the name in question, and with figures even more finely tuned than that: the number before 1986 and the number since then. The fanatic Icelandic care for the purity of the language extends even to people's names. An Icelandic mother cannot call her son Kevin or her daughter Heather. The name book enables prospective parents to pick a suitable Icelandic name for their child. However, they are allowed to create a name out of two different halves. I stayed with people in Akureyri who named their daughter *Eydis* —a combination derived from two traditional names (it means *beautiful island*). I wish I had such a name! *Betty Jane* is a cute name for a little girl, but for an adult, and now an ageing, woman, it's not. I should be *Jana Ingudóttir.*

—YOUR FRIEND, BETTY JANE

CHAPTER TWO

SIGHTSEEING
—LETTER TO MY GRANDFATHER

DEAR AFI:

I have seen much more of Iceland than you had before you left, so I'm sure you'll be interested if I tell you about it.

Before I begin, I must deal with one shock, more stunning than jet lag, and that is the difference between night and day, or rather, the lack of. Is it still night if it isn't dark? Sunrise, sunset, and never the twain shall meet, unless you go high enough till the earth tilts tellingly towards (or away?) and you can see both sides of the sun at the same time. This happened on my first trip to Iceland when, on the same side of the plane, I viewed from one window the sun setting and from the adjacent window the sun rising. I don't have to tell you how long the days are, but I'll tell you, it compounds the jet lag.

We're all creatures of habit and committed to our circadian rhythms. Look at what trouble people seem to have adjusting every spring when they leap forward onto daylight saving time, and in fall totter back onto standard time. I know one person who thinks this is for the sake of the farmers, so that their crops can benefit with the extra hour of sunshine each day!

The best solution to the jet lag problem, I have read, is to go to bed when it's dark in the new location and to rise when it's light. Simple. But what if there isn't enough pale winter light or sufficient summer darkness to guide behaviour, what then? Well, I stayed up all the white night. Oddly enough, I did not sleep half the dark day during my winter visit. Perhaps the festive season contributed to people's wakefulness despite the dark, but when I was there no one I knew went to bed any earlier because of somnolent shadows. Perhaps Icelanders have become casual sleepers like me, who don't really notice the time or the light. Perhaps this is where I get my peculiar sleeping habits. Actually, I like to sleep in the light, I mean in daylight. It reassures me because I think that even if I am asleep, someone else is awake and watchful. I didn't mind being awake for such long hours during the summer weeks I was in Iceland; I read a book every night and napped on the tour bus if I needed it. The darkness in the winter was trickier to get used to. Terms like afternoon and evening have no meaning in a place where winter daylight lasts fewer than two hours.

By the time I arrived at Hofsos on Skagafjerði, I was used to the darkness, sort of, but it still amazed me. On December 20, we (Lorna, Terry and I) had a late breakfast with kin and came outside about ten minutes to noon just as the sun was rising. We went with a cousin of your grandson Terry's to sit and talk at his place and watched the sun set, at ten minutes past one.

That day, I crossed a glacier. It took me a little more than a minute, as I stepped gingerly on the ice in my city boots so I wouldn't slip. This tiny, shiny glacier measures only about two metres across, but who knows how many fathoms deep or how many centuries old it is? One can only assume that it was there when Amma—not my *amma* then—Sigríður Pálsdóttir, at the age of 17, set out from Hofsos on a ship bound for Canada. Maybe she picked her way across it too in boots not so different from my stylish ones, with their laces and high tops.

I went to Iceland that winter for the express purpose of experiencing the shortest day of the year and to glow in all

the lights celebrating the winter solstice. It had been summer when I went before and then I stayed up with the
sun. This time I wanted to see the night. I did, and shivered
my way through the darkness and cold of Glaumbær, the
oldest extant sod farmhouse in Iceland—my goal.

I also basked in the warmth of more relatives and new
friends who shared their Christmas cheer with me as I
coasted on the goodwill and linguistic skill of my Western
Icelandic cousins. I couldn't have asked for better tour
guides, friends and interpreters. Terry and I share one set
of grandparents—that's you and Amma. I'm sure you
remember Terry better than you remember me because
he lived in Gimli all year round and you saw him every day.
The people in Hofsos are connected to the other side of his
family. You remember his mother was a Solmundson? Lara's
family came from around Skagafjörður, one fjord west of
Akureyri, which is on Eyjafjörður. I'm not talking relatives
now, I'm talking glaciers. Afi, I love glaciers! Most especially
I love Vatnajökull, in the southeast of Iceland, the largest
glacier in Europe.

Years ago when I first viewed the Columbia Glacier in the
Canadian Rockies, I dubbed it the Columbia Gravel Pit. I
was sure that Icelandic glaciers would also look like the rear
end of the world. I concluded that, like the promised land,
most glaciers are better viewed from a distance. Up close,
the vision is spoiled by the detritus of a behemoth in (very
slow) motion. The great fat lip of this dirty monopode
curls up and back from the pool of meltwater, leaving a dis-
mal gravel bed that makes landfill look attractive. No
wonder it's called terminal moraine.

Better to view a glacier from afar, I thought—gleaming
white, pristine, silent—or maybe from on top by climbing
onto its groaning, noisy body and slip-sliding over the
blinding surface, but carefully linked with others lest the trip
end in a terminal crevasse. I've never done this and never

plan to, but my alpine son has. That was my attitude before I encountered Vatnajökull.

The best way, and the best glacier to see the best way, is by boat on the ice-blue water at the foot of this breath-taking ice fortress, my favourite glacier in the whole world. Chips off the big block calve like icebergs in microcosm— pretty macro for micro. The pilot of our little sightseeing boat kept careful distance from these beautiful, surreal palaces, floating lazily and lethally on their subaqueous razors. Too close, we could easily have had our keel slit; we probably were too close, but it was worth the risk. We slid past ice sculptures of white and ancient snow with blue shards of sky and crystalline air bubbles fast frozen in their exotic, eroded, convoluted mint-green and sapphire depths. My eyes felt as liquid and cold as the water holding all that beauty. When I turned my gaze to the horizon and our tour bus in the car park, I was totally disoriented, an alien returning reluctantly to Earth.

It took 12 days in a Mercedes-Benz bus to drive up and down and around the entire island on a sometimes rocky and never more than two-lane Ring Road. The last seg-ment of this road was washed away in the fall of 1996 by a flood of melted-glacier water when a volcano erupted under Vatnajökull and filled an underground lake to over-flowing. That volcano erupted again in December, 1998. The full extent of the damage had yet to be determined as I write this to you. The danger of flooding this time is less than it was, but lava ash remains a problem. Anyway, this last, southeastern section of the road, warping through surreal terrain, has still not recovered from the eruption of a volcano three centuries before and is now damaged by the recent eruptions.

Long ago I thought I owed my Icelandic heritage to the eruption of a volcano in the late 19th century, and had thought it a rare event. Not so. The entire island is volatile, with about 200 volcanoes, a lot of them still active. The best-known and the highest one is Mount Hecla (about 4,900 feet or 1,490 metres), which last erupted in 1991. Dyngjufjöll erupted in 1875, covering a huge area in the north and east with volcanic ash and driving people from their homes coincidentally to join an eruption of immigration that sent other disgruntled, hungry Europeans to the New World. If the sheep could have left, they would have too, because Icelandic volcanoes are seldom still and neither sheep nor anything else may safely graze on tentative lichen that takes a hundred years of clawing to soften lava rocks. No one had told me that.

There must be something to this notion of déjà vu. Why else, when I first beheld the iceberg paintings of Lawren Harris in the McMichael gallery in Kleinburg, Ontario, did I catch my breath and sink to the floor to gaze and gaze while sympathetic viewers stepped over and around me? Blue and white, the principal colours of floating icebergs and melting glaciers, dominate my inner landscape. A couple of years ago in Newfoundland, when I visited Canadian writer Joan Clark, she took me to see iceberg calves in the various bays around St. John's. I came away with an unshakeable impression that I had seen live things, as vital and powerful as whales, with a will of their own. The knowledge of their age increases my mystic response. The ice is 10,000 years old, the water frozen in time as clear and pure as ancient crystal springs. I am suspended with it, caught in a dream of blue.

I had a similar feeling of déjà vu in California when, long before I visited Iceland, I stayed with a friend at her beach house on Dillon Beach, north of San Francisco. Every morning we walked on the shore, where the ruggedness of the coastline surprised me. On a bluff behind us a driftwood house perched, overlooking the rocks and ocean below; at least it looked like driftwood. The design was probably an ingenious and expensive architect's idea of rustic simplicity. Every morning I turned to look up at the cliff with its organic house, feeling as if I had seen it before. When I finally saw the coasts of Iceland, I realized why the scene had seemed so familiar. Is that déjà vu or race memory, or what?

Everyone romanticizes scenery: picturesque glaciers, mountains, rocks and water. Everyone loves waterfalls, cataracts, rushing mountain streams, whirlpools, rapids— any kind of water in a hurry. I wonder how many Bridal Veil Falls there are in the world? There's something about rocks and water in its white descent over them that appeals to the poet in all of us, and to photographers as well. With all those rocks and all that ice I should have known that Iceland is spectacularly endowed with waterfalls.

Gullfoss (Golden Falls) is probably the most famous, about 10 kilometres east of geyser country. Geysir, which gave its name to such phenomena all over the world, used to be very regular until some smart ass tourist earlier in this century ruined it by stuffing it full of rocks and dirt to make it spout on demand. Now the big spout regularly requires an enema (soap) to make it perform, so it's not as popular as its smaller companion, Strokkur, which still shoots boiling hot water about 20 metres into the air at three-minute intervals. Nowadays the neighbouring water-fall gets more attention than the geysers. Gullfoss is the breathtaking splash the Hvítá River makes as it drops its load of water 32 metres into the 70-metre-deep, two-and-a-half-kilometre-long canyon below.

About the middle of the 20th century, foreigners almost succeeded in buying the waterfall for hydroelectric development. According to what is now a legend, a neigh-bouring farmer, Tómas, and his daughter, Sigríður Tómasdóttir, succeeded in lobbying against the plan. Sigríður walked to Reykjavík to save the waterfall, threatening to throw herself in if it was destroyed. Happy ending: the government bought the site and turned it into a national park. They even put up a monument to Sigríður above the falls.

This reminds me of a story I was told when I visited New Zealand, about a proposed hydroelectric development that was going to lower the level of a lake that was over a thousand feet deep by some three inches. A massive petition from all over the country—just about the entire population of New Zealand, babies who couldn't sign their names excepted—persuaded the government to find some other means to generate power. Is it only in relatively small islands, where people feel so close to and so responsible for their resources, that this kind of citizens' concern is effective?

Then there's Góðafoss, the falls of the gods, east of Akureyri on the Skájlfandi River in the north. I walked towards it on wet stepping stones, probably part of the improvements put in place for tourists after Eimskip (the Iceland Steamship Company Ltd.) adopted a few of the most beautiful waterfalls in the country because its ships were already named after them. Góðafoss is only 12 metres high, but very broad. It's the one where legend has it that in A.D. 1000 Thorgeir, the local chief and lawspeaker (president) of the Alþing,[1] threw all the carved statues of his old gods into the falls after he officially accepted the Christian faith for Iceland.

My favourite waterfall is Seljalandsfoss, a bridal veil with a difference because one can walk behind and under it, so I did. I swear there was a troll behind me! The falls are on the Seljalandsá River, about 30 kilometres from Skógar, and drop about 40 metres, a thin stream, as falls go, but noisy enough when you're behind it. I've always wanted to walk behind a waterfall. Needless to say, the air was very moist. No wonder trolls are green; their skin is mildewed.

---

1 The name for the first high court or parliament in Europe.

I didn't see Skógafoss, considered to be the most beautiful of Icelandic waterfalls. Sixty metres high, it has Viking treasure hidden behind it, so the legend goes, but of course you can't get behind it. I also missed Dettifoss in the northeast, the largest Icelandic waterfall in volume, with a drop of 44 metres and great hydroelectric-power potential. In fact, the waterfalls of Iceland are an abundant source of power, augmented every year by melting snow from fairly heavy precipitation. I was told that the year before I was in Akureyri, the snow reached the rooftops of all the one-storey houses in the city and people had to tunnel out their front doors—not an uncommon situation.

The first falls I saw, apart from all the nameless tumbling cascades we glimpsed from the highway, was at a well-attended tourist site: Hraunfossar (the *au* in *hraun* is pronounced like the *ai* sound in *chain*). *Fossar* is the plural form of the word for waterfall because a whole bunch of lacy streams weave their way over a bumpy lava ridge down into the Hvítá (white) River, which is blue and white: turquoise blue and the creamy white of the foam. Despite my fear of heights I walked over a narrow stone bridge and looked down at seething water in a cauldron of rocks. This section is called Barnafoss, in memory of some babies who were supposed to have drowned when the original bridge broke. The bairns are forever remembered by twin rainbows—or should I say *hraunbows*?—one on either side of the shattered rock.

I'm pretty fond of volcanoes too (but from a distance). Volcanoes are not to be sneezed at, Afi. Not for nothing has Iceland been called the land of fire and ice: volcanoes and glaciers. Sometimes you get the two put together, as when that volcano erupted under Vatnajökull in 1996 and again in 1998. Hard winters and poor crops may have tempted the people to leave Iceland in the latter years of the 19th century, but the volcanoes must have clinched the decision.

Lava and ash do not become arable for a long, long time. Several generations of stricken farmers and their families can starve while they wait for the lava to yield. Arable land comprises only one-eighth of an island just a little smaller than the island of Newfoundland with, perhaps fortunately for the people dependent on it, about one-half the population. Until well into the 20th century, most people eked out a living raising sheep, farming hay to feed the sheep, and fishing—but they ignored shellfish because they thought they were poisonous, and they didn't catch whales because they didn't have the equipment. (Whale was a bonus when one washed up on shore.) I suppose you knew all this, Afi, did you? You were neither a farmer nor a fisherman so perhaps you did not.

You must have remembered those devastating winters in the 1870s with extreme cold and blizzards, late and early frosts, ruined crops and families driven to the edge of starvation, a condition not unfamiliar to Icelanders over the centuries, but this was worse than usual. Certainly the weather was fierce enough that when the settlers encountered the horrors of winters on the Canadian prairies and considered going back to Iceland, they knew a cold welcome lay in wait. So they stayed. So here I am, thanks to Dyngjufjöll and you.

Rocks mean a lot to Icelanders and to me, too, Afi. Like other northern people who know how terrible it is to get lost, the Icelanders built markers to guide the way of wanderers. In Canada we call such a marker *inukshuk*.[2] *Inukshuks* are quite popular; a Canadian gift catalogue sells a kit to build your own miniature *inukshuk* to be used as a desk ornament or paperweight. Where I live now, in a terrain of rocks and water, a fad has sprung up of building these figures, about three feet high, on low

2 Defined in *The Canadian Oxford Dictionary*: "a figure of a human made of stones, originally used to scare caribou into an ambush, and now used as a marker to guide travellers."

promontories close to the highway. An abundance of rocks makes this possible. The builders are neither Inuit nor Icelanders, as far as I know, but who can resist rocks?

As I understand it, the very first signposts were markers made of small rocks added one at a time at the side of a road or path to indicate where others had passed before. Icelanders piled rocks like this, too, only there were no roads or paths in Iceland, more like trackless waste, a poetic term for a barren land you could get lost in. These markers were casually built over a period of time, less deliberate than cairns. Slow accumulation paid off. I guess no one was in any hurry.

Icelanders also like cairns *(steindys).*[3] Cairns are more serious structures, made of bigger rocks. The first cairn I ever knew by that name was in Gimli, a tall (12 feet) mound of rough stones held together with cement. My brother remembers trying to climb it. Built in 1935 as a project of the Icelandic National League, it commemorated the diamond jubilee of the first landing of the settlers and used rocks from the surrounding beach, including the big one on top—a 25,000-pound red granite boulder. Designed by Dr. A. Blondal and erected by Thorstein Borgfjord, it was unveiled October 21, 1935, by Mrs. N. J. Sommerville (formerly Steinunn Stefansson), a daughter of pioneer parents. Its cornerstone is stuffed with commemorative newspapers: copies of *Framfari, Heimskringla, Lögberg, Sameiningin, Heimir, Breidablik, Almanak* and *Freyja* (the only suffragette newspaper ever published in Canada).

The plan was, you may remember, Afi, for the annual *Fjallkona* (Maid of the Mountain) presiding over Icelandic Celebration Day (Islendingadagurinn) to stop on her way by during the parade and lay a wreath at the cairn in honour of the pioneers. It used to stand in a small fenced-in

---

3 *The Canadian Oxford Dictionary* defines a cairn as a "mound of rough stones used as a monument or landmark."

enclosure at the corner of an open field on Third Avenue, two blocks north of Centre Street. Then the cairn was moved to a more central position so that it was surrounded by the new Gimli Public School. For the last few years no one has been hanging wreaths on it or anything else because the cement is cracking up. An effort is being made to raise enough money to restore it and then the commemorative drive-by will begin again. You can't just ignore a big rock like that.

No one ever told me our beloved rocks were petrified trolls until I visited Iceland. Thereby hangs a tale, Afi, or several.

I also discovered that Iceland is environmentally friendly, using its hydroelectric power instead of fossil fuels. In fact, especially after the oil crisis in the 1970s, Iceland cut down on its import of expensive oil and now its use of that oil is pretty much limited to transportation—for cars and fishing boats. This is possible not only because of the waterfalls but especially because of the geysers, because of the geothermal energy they represent.

The island lies right over the split between the tectonic plates known as the Mid-Atlantic Ridge. In fact, at Thingvellir, the great bluff and valley where the Alþing used to meet, I actually stepped across a small crevasse, no more than a hand span across, which I was told was the beginning of that ridge. One small step for me literally meant one foot in Europe and one in the New World.

Like other plate boundaries, the ridge has a very high heat flow, a temperature gradient ranging from about 50° to 1,500°C, two to five times greater than the average thermal gradient in the rest of the world. Iceland enjoys the last wash of the warm Gulf Stream and, as I discovered, precipitation is heavy. Put these facts together and presto! you have hydro power and geothermal resources like nowhere else in the world, and a good thing too, because Iceland is the world's third highest per capita consumer of energy, which is both inexpensive and keeps things comfortable. The biggest outlay goes for space heating; the second for public swimming pools—year-round, open air—all 120 of them, comprising a total surface area of about 23,000 square metres.

I swam in Akureyri on the day before Christmas during an unprecedented cold spell; the thermometer registered -20°C. The toughest part was hardening my shivering resolve for a sprint in my wet bathing suit across the cement deck to the closer of two hot pools. I didn't have to worry about slipping. I had to move quickly so my feet wouldn't freeze to the concrete. Gratefully I slid into 42° water in a hot whirlpool, where I sat like a placid lobster until I was warm enough to swim. The swimming pool was about 20°C. After 10 or 12 lengths I pulled out and slipped into the other hot pool to finish off at 33°.

All the water used for these pools came out of the earth at something over 70°C, cool for Iceland. (It's cooler in the north.) The heat of the water depends on whether it is taken directly from the underground, in which case it is both incredibly hot and incredibly smelly—sulphur, mostly. A more aesthetic way of supplying hot water is to run clear water over pipes carrying the hot, heavy mineral stuff inside. It works, I guess, a little like my hot line. I pump water from my lake for all my uses except drinking. In the winter I have to turn on a hot line that runs up through the intake pipe and heats the water so it won't freeze on its way to my house.

Akureyri actually uses a heat pump, two of them, installed in 1984, the only district heating system to do so, for economic reasons. They extract heat from some of the return water (at 35°C) and pump another part of the return water back up to 80°.

In the early part of the 20th century, the chief uses of all that hot water and steam were for cooking, bathing and laundry. Not until 1930 was the first hot water piped to houses in Reykjavik for heating purposes. I read that it now costs an average of $300 to heat a house for the winter in Iceland. It takes about 1.6 cubic metres of 800°C water to heat each cubic metre of living space annually. The used water goes into the sewage system at about 350°C, plenty warm enough to be used for the de-icing of pavement as it runs beneath the streets. No salt.

Fascinating as this is, I think the greenhouses are the most interesting part of the story. Almost every new house I saw in Iceland had a little greenhouse attached to it where people experiment with grapes and hibiscus flowers. Out in the country, I could see steam rising from cracks in the earth in the fields—though rarely. More often it has been harnessed, a greenhouse built over the steam and the hot water tapped, either for a hothouse or for heated soil. The most ubiquitous vegetables in Iceland at any meal are delicious hothouse tomatoes and English cucumbers. Since 1920 when the first geothermal heating of greenhouses started, there are now 175,000 square metres under glass while 15,000 square metres of soil are heated by underground pipes. In addition to tomatoes and cucumbers, produce includes mushrooms, peppers, lettuce and eggplants as well as flowers for the domestic market. With artificial lighting increasing the growing season, these greenhouses can now meet local demand for up to six months of the year.[4] I don't think we do any better in Ontario!

Manitoba, where you and Amma ended up, is actually colder than Iceland. I looked up Winnipeg, Gimli and MacTier, Ontario, where I live now, and London, England, Reykjavik and Akureyri in the world atlas because I wasn't sure of their respective latitudes. At MacTier, I'm actually the farthest south at about 45 degrees latitude; London at 50 is

---

4 All the above information culled from Geo-Heat Bulletin Vol. 17, No. 4, on the URL http://www.oit.osshe.edu/admin/geoheat/bulletin/bull17-4/art25/arts5.htm.

a little north of Moosonee, about level with Gimli. Reykjavik looks to be at about 65 and Akureyri is just a smidge south of the Arctic Circle. So which place is coldest? Gimli, Manitoba.

The prairie has no Gulf Stream to waft a warmer draft its way; unrelenting arctic temperatures chill the blood while bitter winds drive great blankets of snow into beautiful, sculpted, lethal drifts. What a place for those hard-driven emigrants to seek out as the promised land! I thought of them—of you and Amma—a lot as I drove north from Reykjavik to Akureyri in the winter. Not only was the climate a little less relentless, comfort was closer at hand. All those steam-emitting fissures in the earth and hot pools had to be a source of warmth. The great poet and scholar Snorri Sturluson had his own private pool, Snorrilaug. Imagine—a private hot tub dating from the 13th century! Nothing like that in Manitoba. At least there was wood around to burn, but you had to melt every drop of water in the winter.

I lie. Gimli had cold running water all year round. I remember from my childhood summers there the artesian wells on every other street corner gushing icy-cold water into my hands when I needed a drink, and you had your own private well in the yard behind the big house. It was my first household chore, to carry drinking water back to the cottage on the same property, and I remember the small pails I was given to handle. The cold water flowed from the wells and ran in ditches alongside the roads and then across the broad sandy beach down into the lake. Even in the heat of summer the water was still painfully cold when I ran across the hot sand and splashed through it—one of my earliest, shivering memories. Later, the wells were capped and had to be pumped to release the water. Later still, the water was piped into the houses and I suppose they use lots of water-softening chemicals.

Isn't it odd? Water sprang hot from the earth in one country and cold in another. It must have been almost like arriving at another planet, Afi, and must have been yet another shock for the immigrants to get used to. It's not a bad metaphor, either, for all the change you experienced.

You have to remind me, too, how scarce wood is in Iceland. I know it wasn't always. The earliest settlers, the Norwegian Vikings who first settled Iceland, between 874 and 930, used the best of the indigenous birch for their ships and burned the rest for fuel. The birch may have been among the reasons they moved to Iceland in the first place. For centuries now, however, wood has been sorely lacking as a building material. When I first came to visit, I thought that the 45-minute drive from the airport at Keflavik to Reykjavik, where almost half of Iceland's 270,000 people live, made the dark side of the moon look inviting, not that I've seen the dark side of the moon. We passed over an ancient, timeless, unforgiving, barren landscape, long since devastated by lava and ash, and I fell in love with it. *Vík,* I learned, means bay; *kefla* is swamp; *reyk* is smoke. I read that when those long-ago sailors first saw the site they thought the vapours rising from the steam fissures in the earth were smoke so they called it Smoky Bay—*Reykja-vík*. Today, the steam and hot water is capped and the city is probably one of the world's most smoke-free urban environments.

Reykjavik,[5] old as it is, is a modern city where old meets temporary. Everything looks makeshift. Evidently lava rocks are unsuitable building material and there are, as I said, no longer trees in Iceland. A massive tree-planting program, bringing in Alaska pines and birches, has barely begun to have an effect. In the not-so-long-ago olden days, houses were made of sod. Sod doesn't last as long as stone. Later houses made of corrugated iron rusted almost instantly.

---

5 I am not using the accent on *vik,* because Reykjavik is an international name.

Not until the 20th century, when poured concrete and concrete blocks were developed, have any buildings lasted more than 50 years, with stucco finishes that require frequent patching and painting. The oldest commercial building in Reykjavik was built in 1855 (by your grandfather, Robert Tergesen!). When I saw it, it had just been made a Heritage building, simply for the virtue of lasting that long. At the time, the city fathers were planning to remove the large front windows and restore it to its original ugly appearance.

Before I move on with my memories, Afi, I want to return to Hofsos for one last look. I have already mentioned Terry's kin on his mother's side. We had a visit and dinner on the horse farm with Valgarður Þorhállsson (Valdi) and Valgerður Kristjánsdóttir (Didda) and their children and grandchildren. Then their son, Valgeir Valgarðursson, took us into town and put us up for the night in a spanking-new bed-and-breakfast place that he had just finished building.

Valgeir is a carpenter and entrepreneur. He built that B&B and owns another, older building that he also renovated for travellers. He was about to tear down a house closer to the harbour but changed his mind when he discovered, buried in the earth surrounding it, a seawall: massive, piled stones dating from at least a hundred years earlier—a real find! Valgeir repaired the wall and the house and it's now a restaurant run by his sister. That was his first restoration.

Next he turned his attention to an old warehouse, built by a Danish merchant in the days when Denmark still owned Iceland, and I mean "owned" because Denmark had an economic stranglehold on Iceland's trade. The building is made of heavy dark timber imported from the mainland to this wood-poor island. The upper loft of the structure now hosts summer concerts while the main floor serves as a small, catchall museum, not only historical but natural: one end wall displays some of the birds indigenous to Drángey, the island at the mouth of the fjord. They were stored away when we toured the premises, to protect the taxidermist's handiwork from mice.

Do you remember the story about Drángey? The island is still uninhabited except by birds, thousands of them. It's also dangerous, a craggy, sheer place presenting terrible hazards over the years to birders going after the coveted fowl and their eggs. Many climbers fell to injury or death. Trolls or dark spirits were suspected in these so-called accidents because the ropes that held the birders were not old but frequently showed evidence of cutting. In the 12th century, the story goes, the people called in a bishop to bless the island in the hope of preventing further mishaps. The bishop did what he could, going around, duly anointing the rocks and blessing the cliffs. But on the last sheer rock face, he found his rope was hanging by one strand while a voice warned him to cease his blessing, so he quit. That area is called Heathen Cliff and there are more birds there than anywhere else on Drángey, but few people dare to go over the edge.

Grettir the Strong, hero of a fascinating saga, spent the last year of his life on Drángey. At Christmas dinner in Akureyri, my hostess, Sigrún Björgunsdóttir, told me in simple English (so much more fluent than my Icelandic!) a tale about Grettir on the island while her family smiled encouragement and nodded in pleasure. His servant, she said, had let the fire go out so Grettir swam to shore to bring back fire—a whole sea mile, considered quite a feat—and so was Sigrún's tale. Everyone in Iceland knows the sagas. Did you, Afi? I wish we had talked.

All the building projects I have described were logical steps on the way to Valgeir's major work: the Emigration Museum. On the other side of that little glacier at Hofsos, facing the water, he restored and enlarged the tiny office building where emigrants registered to leave the country. Here is the record honouring the resolute emigrants who left Iceland during the 1870s. It's sort of like Ellis Island in reverse: not the arrival, but the departure is being marked. Valgeir designed a "leaving wall" to greet viewers on entering. It bears a collage of reproductions of emigrants' passports. The basement level of the building is a replication of the kind of ship's hold where the passengers spent so many weeks on their gruelling journey to the promised land.

The government of Iceland engaged the services of a museum curator, Sigríður Sigurðardóttir, who is also the director of Glaumbær Museum, to gather artifacts, mementoes and documents relevant to the departing colonists. She says it's fascinating to discover what the emigrants chose to take with them. I found this idea intriguing. I am interested in their written records, especially women's diaries, but I never thought of the *things* they packed.

So what did they bring along with them? Well, they took books. To that primitive land where hardship awaited them, being literate Icelanders, they took books. Lord Dufferin, Governor General of Canada, would later visit the first immigrants in New Iceland and comment on this fact, that, despite their poverty and deprivation, they all possessed, and read, books. Accustomed as they were to winter darkness, they knew they needed light. Sigríður told me that an item that impressed her was a lantern. It was logical. Someone had the forethought to carry along the means of light to a dark, empty, uninhabited land. We take it all for granted now: light to keep the darkness at bay, heat to keep our bodies comfortable, enough food—we know adequate food is always a problem—but who would have thought of taking light to read by? If you want to read in the dark, certainly you must have light. What other items did the settlers consider essential? Some of the first letters back home included urgent messages to bring rope, lots of rope. What else?

That museum at Hofsos, by the way, opened on *Jónsmessa,* John the Baptist Day, the day nearest to the longest day of the year, June 24, 1996. Valgeir had six men working with him to meet that deadline because he wanted and succeeded in having Vigdís Finnboggadóttir officiate at the ceremony, one of her last public acts before her retirement as president of Iceland. Amazingly, this annual summer festival, only a few years old, has attracted five or six thousand tourists every year to Hofsos. In 1998 the first Íslendingadagur was held there the first weekend in August and it may replace the earlier celebration. Most people prefer to go to Iceland in the summer. Not everyone prizes the dark as I do.

You would be interested to know, Afi, that I visited the new heritage museum at the other end of the line, which opened in the newly renovated old Gimli school building in 1997. There I took careful note of the lanterns and various forms of lights the travellers took with them as well as the wooden chests and trunks (realizing how hard that wood was to come by), sturdy enough to withstand the long journey. The tools and utensils are to be expected, but I took a careful look at the fishing nets, boats and sleds, knowing that the men had to learn a different kind of fishing—lake, instead of ocean, with smaller mesh in the nets—and a totally new technique for catching fish through solid ice.

I was impressed with the women's sewing, embroidery and knitting that the museum displayed. This kind of handwork bespeaks hours and hours of evening work once the youngest children had been put to bed and after the housework, the gathering and preparing of food, was done, but still with chores to do, spinning and weaving, sewing and knitting. As on the other side of the ocean, there was in every immigrant family or group a designated reader who kept the needlewomen entertained and awake while they worked. Children might listen, too, until they fell asleep, and then someone would tell them the end of the story in the morning. Older ones, both boys and girls, had a quota of knitting to do.

I don't remember you or Amma reading the sagas but I do remember you reading the newspaper aloud at night, Afi. I remember also being frustrated in my search for something to read. I found a few books by Nellie McClung and several by Horatio Alger. All the other books were in Icelandic and didn't do me any good. Isn't it odd, Afi, that my travels should bring me back to Gimli, where I began? Knowing more than I knew before, appreciating more, I come full circle back to the "home of the gods," Gimli.

Now the questions begin to arise: How could people live in that country? I mean Iceland, but one might as well ask it of Canada. And why? For beauty? For hot springs and cold lakes, green meadows and black mountains, reckless waterfalls and relentless glaciers, fire and ice? Those are reasons? I think people stay, have stayed, not for the carefree lightening of the spirits for almost twenty-four hours on a summer's day, but for the darkening assertion of the spirit in the gloom of the winter-long night. I began to imagine those people huddling together in their sod houses in the darkness, telling each other stories to keep terror at bay, or maybe to evoke it, deliciously, and then, finally, writing them down, to last, on leather pages bound in scarce wood. I had to see that for myself. It's a sight worth seeing.

—YOUR LOVING GRANDDAUGHTER, BETTY JANE

CHAPTER THREE

EMIGRANTS
—LETTER TO MY BROTHER'S GRANDSON

Travel light, they say, all travellers must
shed weight, divest themselves of excess
in the way of burdens, detritus of a life.
Weigh possibilities.
Lighten the load but carry memory in secret
dark and secret pockets. Heaving chest
on board with tools to implement a life,
clothes, food to keep a life
precious little else
little that's precious.
Books, yes books, a must
impossible without, no mould
no rust, keep inner life alight
keep shadows at bay shed light
Light, yes, light.
Don't pack shadows, shadows follow
so take light, a lantern
to light the dusty way
to light.

BJW

DEAR GUÐMUNDUR AARON:
You are more Icelandic than anyone in my family and
didn't even know it. On your mother's side you have an
Icelandic great-grandmother and a passel of great-great-

grandparents; your father is Icelandic, both sides, and still lives in Iceland. If I were good at arithmetic I could tell you what percentage Icelandic that makes you, but I'm not so I can't. When I met you for the first time this past winter, I found that you were unaware of most of these connections and knew little about our family history, or Iceland's.

I guess when I was your age (20) I didn't know much, either, although a little more than you, because of going to Gimli in the summer. Afi, Uncle Pete, Uncle Joe and Uncle Robby welcomed me back every year with a gruff nod, saying goodbye at Labour Day with another gruff nod and a dollar bill for a treat. That was worth a kiss—on the cheek, most of them rather stubbly, as I remember. Everything I've learned about my origins I learned as an adult and most of the information has come only recently when I started asking questions and filling in the blanks. Afi and Amma came from Iceland, that's about all I knew.

My grandfather, Afi—Hans Pjetur Tergesen—your great-grandfather, was not, however, among the vanguard of emigrants, nor did he suffer the way the early pioneers did; in fact, he was not a pioneer but an entrepreneur. I didn't know this. All I knew was that he lived in a big three-storey house on Fourth Avenue in Gimli, with its own artesian well on the property and a stand of pine trees wonderful for climbing and forts, and a woodpile wonderful for climbing and forts, and a barn never used for horses in my memory but wonderful for climbing and forts. The property went so far back, it allowed my brother, Jack (your grandfather), to make a tennis court one year and another year to dig a hole to China. Uncle Joe and his wife Lára and their two sons (one of them my dear cousin Terry, your first cousin, twice removed) lived year round in the house next door, and my family summered in the cottage next to that, which was, I later discovered, Afi's wedding present to my parents. In fact, Afi owned the whole block.

Uncle Robby built a city-style house across the street from the Big House; two other cousins spent their summers in cottages at the other end.

When I was engaged to be married and suddenly interested in silver and china patterns, I turned over Amma's silver and the china at Sunday dinner one day to discover that it was Birks sterling silver (Tudor Plain) and Limoges china (white). I had never noticed before. When Afi died, his son Jóhann (Joe) took over the store. My parents went to Europe twice on money received from the sale of his birch land north of Gimli, proceeds from which were divided equally among the six surviving children. (Amma bore seven children in all, but one died as an infant.)

Afi was a successful man, a town councillor; mayor of Gimli three or four times. These facts filtered through. I didn't know that he loved theatre and played roles in amateur theatrics, first produced in the upper loft of the store. An older cousin told me this but she couldn't remember any of the plays, only that she laughed a lot. He was stubborn, everyone said so, but even I could see that he could be swayed by a word or a smile from Amma. He used to shoo children away from the toy department in the store—one crowded display table—and then he would fiddle with the mechanical toys until they broke and he muttered about shoddy workmanship. He used to hum a little tune under his breath when he did this and my cousin Terry and I have been trying to recall it.

Afi planned ahead, always. He differed from most of the emigrants in that he had a trade: he was a tinsmith. He could earn a living. He met Amma on the ship, I know, and spent, so he claimed, his last dollar on the marriage certificate, but somehow I doubt that it was his last dollar. He didn't move up to New Iceland (Nyja Ísland), specifically, to Gimli, right away. Although the worst was over—the smallpox and the soul-crunching adjustment to the harsh conditions—he didn't go there right away. Instead, after marrying Amma in Winnipeg he moved to Churchbridge, Saskatchewan, for a brief time and then back to Winnipeg, where he set up a tinsmith business with a partner. He stayed there until he made enough money to have the store built in Gimli so that it was all ready and waiting for him and his growing family. That's how it happened that my mother, your great-grandmother, was born in Winnipeg. I always wondered.

Afi moved into his general store in 1899 some 24 years after the first settlers landed on Willow Island. Like them, he never looked back, but for a different reason. He didn't need to. It was to become H. P. Tergesen & Sons because it turned out that he had male descendants willing to carry on. He sent away to Chicago for plans for the house and built it in 1908 on Fourth Avenue, out of the centre of Gimli where the store was. I can pick out the house in early pictures, way out there in the background. I remember he had the biggest rain barrel in the world in the basement so that between it and the artesian well, the house was fully supplied with water. He had the house wired for electricity though it would be 22 years before electric power reached Gimli and he could turn on the lights. He built a windmill on the roof of the barn, hoping to supply auxiliary power to the house. The first sentence I ever learned in Icelandic I heard almost daily from him until I finally asked Amma what it meant: *"mylun hefur ekki pumpa ydag."* She laughed out loud when she heard it, and translated: "The mill hasn't pumped today."

I wrote a play about Afi—about Amma, really—about a pioneering family that came to Gimli and put down roots in a new land—quite sentimental. I called the play *Veranda* because it took place on the veranda of the big house, and I said airily that I hadn't let fact interfere with fiction, and I hadn't. I still didn't know that much, which was probably just as well, for I was after a different kind of truth. I was really trying to understand my grandmother. I had the character Petur say, at one point, "I never really knew her." I still believe that. I am, as you will learn, Aaron, interested to the point of obsession in women's stories.

Since this is all new to you, I'm going to go back two millennia to the first Settlement, the immigration to Iceland of the first Norse settlers. If you already have some idea of how literate the Icelanders are, and how careful they are with their records, you won't be surprised to learn of the *Landnamabók*, Book of Settlements, or I would say the book of first settlement. Written in the 12th century, it reports on the people who first settled in Iceland. Of course, it names names.

But first a few transients came to the island, some Irish monks who actually lived there a hundred years earlier. A small stone carving of a man with a cross on his chest has been found in Greenland, dating from the 8th century. These first settlers may have been routed by the next "invasion" for they are supposed to have departed so quickly they left behind a few books and bells.

Next, in the 9th century, a Norwegian explorer named Naddodd on his way to the Faroe Islands was blown off course to find a new land mass in his way—the east coast of Iceland. Cold and empty the land seemed, and it was snowing on the mountains as he sailed away, so Naddodd called it Snaeland (Snowland). Gardar Svavarsson from Sweden sailed around the land mass and discovered that it was a big island. He and his crew wintered in the north part of the island, building houses to survive, so they called their harbour Husavík (House Bay). There's still a village there. When Gardar left the following summer he called the place Gardarsholmi (Gardar's Island).

Then Floki Vilgerdarson decided to come, with friends and kin and three ravens, intending to live in Gardarsholmi.

No dates are given for these early forays; we know they must have taken place before the permanent settlement in 874. Floki's use of the ravens was like Noah's use of the doves on the ark. He sent out a raven to see if the land was close; the bird always returned. Finally, a raven flew out and didn't come back, so Floki followed it ("Follow that raven!") and settled on a fjord on the northwest side. The tourists had a good summer with plenty of fish and ducks' eggs but they forgot to prepare for winter. With no hay, their stock died and they almost did too. In the spring Floki looked over the land from the top of a nearby mountain and saw another fjord, full of ice, on the other side. He called it Isafjorður (Icefjord) and called the whole place Ísland (Iceland). This time the name stuck.

At last, according to the *Landnamabók*, along came Ingólfur Árnarson, a chieftain from Norway, with his family and entourage, arriving in 874. The story goes that he threw some logs from the ship into the water to help him decide where to land. I've read several different versions of this legend: one, they were just sticks; two, they were "sacred wood"; three, they were the legs of his throne. The point is not where he found the wood, but why and where it fetched up. I think he had discovered a good method of testing the tides and currents and making sure there were no shoals or reefs to deflect or break the wood. Anyway, Ingólfur (everyone in Iceland is always called by the first name) built his farm on the Smoky Bay—so-called because of the "smoke" that hung in the air above the site. It was steam, actually, from the underground thermal activity.

Over the next 60 years other Viking settlers came, bringing some Celts with them, probably slaves acquired in raids, and settled in habitable areas around the coast. By the year 930 a law code was accepted. Four local courts ran the country in between the annual sessions of the Supreme Court or parliament, the Alþing, which met for two weeks once a year at Thingvellir and which was attended by a substantial representation of the population. It was at the Alþing that Christianity was officially adopted, in the year 1000, making Iceland the only country in the world to legislate the new religion. That was a millennium milestone.

Two horrendous events in history have made it relatively simple to track people's families. One was an outbreak of bubonic plague (two outbreaks, actually) in the 15th century that reduced the population of Iceland by half, in fact, to about four traceable clans. The other event was an exceptionally vicious volcanic eruption in the 18th century that destroyed so much arable land that people starved to death, decimating the population. Later, towards the end of the 19th century, another eruption sent about 15,000 people to seek other homes in the new world—again about one-tenth of the population of Iceland at that time, not as dramatic an event as the earlier catastrophes, and perhaps without such far-reaching effects on the inhabitants remaining, but certainly with a lasting effect on us. We Western Icelanders wouldn't be here if it hadn't been for that major exodus.

By 1100 the population is thought to have reached a peak of about 70 or 80 thousand people. In the 18th century it sank below 40,000 three times. It was slowly reaching the numbers achieved in the 12th century when the mass exodus at the end of the 19th century brought it down again. Today the population is about 270,000 people, with nearly one-half of them living in Reykjavik. Compare this, Aaron, to a current (high) estimate of 90,000 Western Icelanders living in North America. Theirs, as you may know from a smattering of North American historic lore, was the second settlement in the New World.

I suppose we can't really count the casual visits made by Leif Eiriksson (Leif the Lucky) and his contemporaries in the

10th century as settlements. Again, they happened because someone was blown off course. Leif's father, Eirik the Red, had been banished from Iceland for manslaughter and settled in Greenland with his family and followers. In 985-86 a sailor, Bjarni Herjólfsson, on his way to Greenland, lost his bearings and ended up somewhere along the coast of Labrador, or maybe Newfoundland. Encouraged by the man's descriptions, not only of the route but also of the resources (salmon, game, lumber for ships), Leif organized an expedition to this new land in 995-96. This and later trips are described in *The Vinland Sagas*. As you may be aware, Aaron, the base camp (Leifsbuðir) has been excavated and restored at L'Anse aux Meadows on the north side of Newfoundland.

It's not fully clear why Leif's people didn't stay—no longer than three years. Perhaps the fact that the land was already occupied (by the now extinct Beothuk tribe) deterred them, or perhaps there was something internal going on, as the writer Joan Clark surmises in her novel, *Eiriksdottir*, about the last expedition led by Leif's sister, Freydís Eiriksdóttir. At any rate, another first was established: the first child born to Europeans on the North American continent—in Newfoundland—was Snorri Þorbrandsson. The next Icelander to be born in Canada did not arrive until 1875.

Nyja Ísland was not the first official settlement by Icelanders in North America. Twenty years earlier, in 1855, the first pioneers arrived in Spanish Fork, Utah, pushing handcarts. I've heard of going to hell in a handcart; the expression must date from the gruelling ordeal settlers experienced pushing all their worldly goods across the prairies in a cart. These Icelanders were Mormons, welcomed to Utah by President Brigham Young of the Church of Jesus Christ of the Latter-Day Saints, which had sent missionaries to Europe to bring new sheep into the fold.

One of them had found new flock members in a pair of Icelanders in Denmark, there to learn a trade. Converted, both to a new religion and a new land, they returned to Iceland and persuaded their families to join the Church and move. They not only prospered in the New World, they also multiplied, aided and abetted, not to say augmented, by Mormon polygamy. Their names are still preserved and honoured on Iceland Day in Utah; the first one was celebrated on the first Saturday in August (3), 1897, a date coinciding with an annual holiday in the Westmann Islands where the original settlers came from. They still commemorate the arrival; in this century three descendants of the original settlers have been honoured with Iceland's Order of the Falcon. They were Kate B. Carter, Johm Y. Bearnson and Byron Geslison.

The reasons for that first small emigration were religious but the departure inspired others. A group of Icelandic farmers began to think of emigrating to the New World, not necessarily North America. The reasons for this exodus are more complicated. Until the middle of the 10th century, Iceland was almost feudal in outlook,[1] and very simplistic. Basically, there were three classes: public functionaries, pastors and farmers. A domestic service law in effect since 1490 obligated everyone to live on a farm, thus guaranteeing jobs and homes and ensuring cheap labour for the landowners. However, this prevented people from striking out on their own and forming settlements in other areas.

The country's economy was agrarian; the standard of living was in direct proportion to agricultural production, and limited. Even today, land devoted to agriculture and under permanent cultivation amounts to 1.1 percent of the total area of the island. When the population went

---

1 The following information is taken from a series of articles published in the Icelandic Canadian newspaper, *Logberg-Heimskringla*, March 6 - April 10, 1998, by permission from *Morgunblaðið*, the Icelandic newspaper in Reykjavik.

up, living standards went down: more people meant less food. It seemed that after that rare peak in the 12th century, every time the population hit 50,000 some disaster occurred to cull the flock: illness (bubonic plague, twice), physical disaster (volcanic eruptions), animal troubles (the "sheep scab disaster"), weather calamities (horrendous winters). The worst of the hardships was known simply as "The Hardship of the Mist" in 1783-86. I gather this was something like a never-ending smog, a mixture of floating lava ash and fog, very hard on the lungs and stock. This seemed to mark a turning point, after which the population began steadily to increase. One historian thinks it was no coincidence that the Mormon Icelanders left the Westmann Islands just as the 60,000th Icelander was born.

Gradually, (relatively) good times made possible an increase in farm production and cultivation in the highlands at the same time as farms were divided into smaller units. However, as the population grew, another shortage of land, and hence of food, became increasingly apparent. Finally, in the winter of 1859-60, faith in the future died along with the stock. A few farmers from Þingeyjarsysla met at Einarsstaðir in Reykjadalur to discuss emigration. Greenland was suggested and rejected as a lateral step to a climate worse than the one they wanted to leave. One man present at the meeting, Einar Ásmundsson, could speak a little Portuguese and had some information about Brazil. At that time, the New World, both North and South America, was actively promoting settlement (hence the Mormons), and Brazil was no exception, promising warm weather and greater independence, that is, their own seemingly unlimited land, with a guarantee of regular steamship service from Germany for emigrants. About 200 people joined an association prepared to explore the idea of emigration.

Well, Aaron, as you might expect, there was a good deal of heated argument, pro and con, both political and personal. Being human, and Icelanders, they were not always in agreement. The winds of change were also blowing in Europe and though they didn't reach the gale force of the French Revolution, nevertheless by the time they reached Iceland, independence was a fresh breeze and a common goal. (Remember that until 1944, Iceland was under Danish rule, having been taken over from Norway in 1380.) Then physical problems rose to thwart the would-be emigrants, chief among them being the lack of a ship. Plans kept falling through and it was not until the winter of 1863 that the first Icelander left for Brazil, followed in the summer by three others. All four men were members of the Emigration Association and one of them at least went for the express purpose of finding suitable farmland for a colony.

For want of a ship the colony in Brazil might have been much larger. Although the Emigration Association numbered as many as 500 people as late as 1873, transportation was proving to be impossible. Finally, about 30 Icelanders went to Copenhagen on their own and sailed from there to South America. By that time, others were leaving for the United States and Canada, which was an easier move in terms of distance and cost.

Be aware, Aaron, that it is for the sake of Western Icelanders everywhere in the New World that I am offering this capsule history. Genuine scholars and historians have published entire books about the great move out of Iceland, when about one-fifth of the population left the country within the space of a few years, beginning in 1875. What remains of the utmost interest to me and, I'm sure, to other Western Icelanders is that their assimilation into their adopted country, while complete, has nevertheless left them with distinctive characteristics and deep roots in another world, invisible but with astonishing tensile strength. Was it the Icelandic climate or Icelandic stubbornness?

Between 1875 and 1879 Nova Scotia also received immigrants from Iceland, although *received* is perhaps too strong a word. The 30 or so Icelandic families who formed a colony there near the Cariboo gold mines didn't stay. The Icelandic newspaper, *Morgunbladið*, reports that a book on the Cariboo gold mines was published in 1990, with one chapter about the Icelandic Colony, covering their disastrous eight years there. Struggling with bad land and eking out a living in the mines with inadequate tools, the Icelanders, whose total numbers are not known, left.

Muskoka, Ontario, was the site of another short-lived disaster. This is the area where I live now and I can tell you, Aaron, the topsoil at its deepest is about the length my little finger and lies on bedrock. Corn, if I ever tried to grow it, would reach about as high as an elephant's toenail. The chief product, besides tourists, is rock. The area also discouraged the Icelanders to cluster in a settlement. Bear in mind, too, that wherever they went, these Icelandic farmers didn't know much about the kind of farming that had to be tackled in North America. Back home, they were used to farming hay, for their sheep; it even took them a couple of centuries to get around to growing a few hardy vegetables. Trees are still sparse in Iceland today, in spite of massive, ongoing tree-planting efforts. An abundance of anything other than rocks, ash and lava was not something these people were used to dealing with. One of the most staggering surprises they encountered in Canada was a wealth of trees, more than they could name, and they didn't even own axes. The land had to be cleared first before they could even begin to grow hay, let alone vegetables. Even when/if the trees were cleared, they probably realized that rocks and stones would not provide a fertile environment for crops. So the survivors of the

115 disappointed would-be Muskokans moved east to join a small, dismayed group in Kinmount, Ontario.[2] This venture turned out to be an even bigger disaster.

The Kinmount settlement was another attempt, doomed from the start, to establish a base, this time with a larger number of hardy souls. Not hardy enough. Reports of the death toll that winter vary, but the estimate was about one in ten, the majority being children—16 of them died within the first three weeks of their arrival. The adults who died were mostly older people. Lillian Vilborg MacPherson's grandfather was one of the children who eluded death in Kinmount and she realizes what a miracle that was. About 350 people left Iceland in September 1874 and arrived in Kinmount, Ontario, that October—not a great choice of season at the best of times and records indicate that the ensuing winter was a killer.

The government put up log barracks as temporary housing for the immigrants. These were inadequate, so two more were built, and barely heated with "boiler ovens" which were to be paid for by the settlers, though the government picked up the shipping costs. Winter employment was promised to the men, work on a new railroad, with the expectation of acquiring land in the spring along with some assistance in tree-clearing and house-building. Overcrowding, unsanitary conditions, disease, hunger, exhaustion and harsh winter conditions killed off the weakest of the colonists, already debilitated by the long journey. Many of them had not recovered from various stomach ailments suffered during the ocean voyage. To top it off, the railway company lowered the wages and then laid off workers. Reporting home in a letter, one of the group commented with admirable understatement that the land didn't

2 I have culled this historical information from articles in *Logberg-Heimskringla*, one published May 1, 1998, by Donald E. Gislason; the other, February 6, 1998, by Lillian Vilborg MacPherson, with their kind permission.

look great. He warned people not to come just yet. After nine months of nightmare, the Kinmount survivors left to go farther west.

Almost no memory or marks remain of the ill-fated Kinmount settlement. None of the deceased was buried in town or in church cemeteries; they were laid in unmarked graves along the banks of the Crego River—perhaps. Even this much is not certain. The Icelandic National League has given approval to the Icelandic Canadian Club of Toronto (ICCT) to go ahead with a Kinmount Memorial to honour the dead. Guðrun Sigursteinsdóttir Girgis has been commissioned to create a sculpture in limestone. ICCT is hoping for official Ontario Heritage plaques to be set on a limestone base on one side of which the settlement story will be written in Icelandic, English and French, with a map of Iceland on the other side. The hope is to dedicate the memorial on July 31, 2000.

Once they arrived in Winnipeg, the beleaguered immigrants were allotted land outside the boundaries of what was then the "postage stamp" province of Manitoba. The biggest attraction seems to have been the fact that the colony could be both autonomous and homogenous: Nyja Ísland (New Iceland) would be exclusively Icelandic. The lake (Winnipeg) was big (13th largest in the world) and would provide fish. There were trees for building houses—and for back-breaking clearing. The government offered assistance and forgiving loans. The catch was the settlers had to live there, no easy matter.

At first no help had been forthcoming to assist the Kinmount survivors in their move from Ontario to New Iceland. Canada's deal was with immigrants coming from their homes across the ocean. These people were already here and had merely changed their minds. Why should they get any more help? Lord Dufferin, then Governor

General of Canada, intervened on their behalf and arranged for a grant to help them move. He had visited Iceland some 20 years earlier and had been impressed with the people. He noticed then and later, the high incidence of literacy among the people.

A word about Churchbridge, Aaron, where your great-grandfather sojourned briefly. The first Icelanders to move to Saskatchewan moved there from Winnipeg in 1885. From Churchbridge they spread to form other communities at Tantallon, Calder, Foam Lake, Leslie, Elfros, Mozart, Wynyard, Kandahar and Dafoe. In July 1988, the Icelandic Canadian Club of Saskatchewan erected a memorial in honour of its pioneers.

Back in Iceland, the emigration groups still held conflicting opinions about their destinations in the New World. The American-bound contingent was divided mainly between Wisconsin, which some people left to join the colony in Manitoba, and Nebraska. Other emigrants briefly considered Alaska, but that was simply jumping from one cold place to another. To those who didn't know any better, Nova Scotia was still a possibility, seeming to offer a better deal. Some of the Kinmount settlers, about 80 in all, actually turned back and moved to Mooseland (Markland) near Halifax, in late winter of 1875, joined by a few disgruntled people from Wisconsin and a few more from Iceland. That failed, too, with unsuitable land and poor working conditions, so that by 1881-82 almost all of these 35 families moved west.

Every year now the Icelandic National League in Gimli stages a "Walk to the Rock" on October 21, the date the first Icelandic settlers landed on Willow Island in 1875. It's not a marathon, just a stroll south on the beach, part way on a paved walk, laid on top of a stone breakwater built to prevent further erosion of the shoreline by stormy, shallow

Lake Winnipeg, and then on to the point where the walkers can now walk on a causeway (built in the 1950s) to Willow Island and think long thoughts before they go back to be rewarded with cookies and hot chocolate. The settlers should have been so lucky.

It hadn't been easy getting there, the last part being the hardest when they attempted to move down the Red River on freight barges never intended to carry people, along with their goods. They had few chattels. There was no hay for the livestock. The captain of a Hudson Bay steamer was enlisted to pull the barges and they made it to Willow Island in good weather, which lasted till the next day. Anyone who thinks Icelandic stubbornness is a bad trait can think again and wonder at the strength it imbues. It's all in the sagas, Aaron. I'll get to them.

Jón Jóhannsson, New Iceland's first baby, was born on Willow Island two days later in a borrowed Hudson's Bay tent. By chance, I spoke recently to that baby's grand-daughter's husband. He raises Icelandic sheepdogs in Gimli, and I am interested in owning one. Small world, New Iceland.

The most significant thing about the move to Manitoba was the right to self-government. The settlers hammered out a constitution for the Republic of New Iceland and formed their own parliament with elected members. Every male[3] over 18 years old with good standing in the community—not property, just a good name—was entitled to vote and was responsible for certain duties: community tasks and the equivalent of taxes for social services (care of widows and orphans, for example). There was a council for arbitration of disputes but there was no penal code, for the simple reason that no one expected to need one. The colonists had a school going within the first twelve months and a newspaper in the second, both perpetuating their language and

---

3 If this sounds like a step back for the women, it was, and they were not long in doing something about it.

culture, but at the same time teaching the people about the new country they found themselves in. Never mind the cold, the human spirit was alive and glowing, and this, in spite of one of the worst Manitoba winters on record the first year and an outbreak of smallpox in the second.

Framfari—meaning "Progress"—is the name of the newspaper, which was published about three times a month for two years, from September 10, 1877, to September 7, 1878, and from October 5, 1878, to January 30, 1880, for a total of 75 issues numbering 298 pages (plus one last gasp, not considered part of the set, published April 10, 1880). Three men were largely responsible for its existence: Sigtryggur Jónasson, the father and leader of the colony; his brother-in-law Jóhann Briem, and Friðjón Friðriksson. Sigtryggur was the unnamed editor of the first eight issues; then Halldór Briem took over the editing although Sigtryggur continued to write for the paper. It was written in Icelandic, as you would expect, in fact, its launch was delayed while the publishers waited for Icelandic fonts to go with their printing press and equipment. Paper was always in short supply and the quality of newsprint very poor, so that fewer than four or five complete sets of the paper survive. Circulation at its peak reached about 600, with many copies going to Iceland.

The Icelandic National League gave me a handsome leather-bound copy of *Framfari,* as a gift for a speech I gave at a national conference. The volume is about the size of one volume of the *Encyclopaedia Britannica.* I read the whole thing, the 298 pages of the original newspaper amounting to 748 pages, double columns. Of course, the original was in Icelandic but I'm happy to say the material is translated[4] because I am not the only member of a later generation who hasn't learned the language. The settlers

---

4 The translator was Professor George Houser, Gimli Chapter, Icelandic National League.

were urged, however, to learn English and most numbers included English summaries of the contents. Aaron, it's fascinating reading! The contents are remarkable.

You might say they are eclectic, ranging from instructions for making fishing nets to storing potatoes, with recipes for homemade bread and fish soup, suggested treatments and medication for diphtheria and scarlet fever, as well as remedies for mosquito bites, teething and poison ivy, with a method for getting rid of mosquitoes. The pages feature stories, anecdotes, poetry both original and translated (from Lord Byron, for example), and riddles and jokes. The Canadian postal system is discussed, with statistics; the tariff on the Canadian dollar explained; and the names and attendance record at Mrs. Lára Pjetursdóttir's school at Gimli are reported. There are history and geography lessons about the readers' adopted country, and news not only of Canada and the United States but also of Iceland and the world, including Russia and China. By far the most ink was spent on religious discussion, specifically the choice of pastor and church for the new community, with enough discussion to cause me to think that the annual Alþing back in Iceland must have been a lively and verbose forum of public opinion. The behaviour of the entire community of New Iceland, in fact, made me aware both of what the people brought with them, revered and as little changed from the old ways as possible, and of what they wished to change, and did. They had so much to learn, and wanted to.

The irony is that of all the places the immigrants chose for their major settlement, the shores of Lake Winnipeg were probably the least promising, financially speaking. The smaller contingents in the United States prospered more on an economic basis. Yet Gimli and the surrounding communities are the ones with the most distinctive voice, even as they have been assimilated within Canada. Today,

Islendingadagurinn (Icelandic Celebration Day) attracts 40 to 50 thousand visitors to Gimli every year. It has become a focal point of all the Western Icelanders in North America, whose allegiance to their heritage transcends national (Canadian /U.S.) boundaries. Gimli has become a mecca for extended families who use the festival as an excuse for reunions running to as many as 500 people, often wearing distinctive matching sweatshirts bearing family names and marching proudly in the parade, carrying the babies and pushing the old folks in their wheelchairs. Everyone, it seems, including you and me, Aaron, has a Gimli in the soul.

—YOUR GREAT-AUNT B.J.

CHAPTER FOUR

THE GENE POOL
—LETTER TO MY DAUGHTER

DEAR KATE:

You are the right person to direct this letter to, my dear daughter, because it looks as if you have some of the instincts of a family archivist. I suppose that's because you emigrated from your homeland and you actually prize what you no longer have more than your siblings who stayed put. In any case, it's a pleasure to write to you because we think alike about a lot of things.

I suppose when one lives in a country where one knows almost all the people by name, and their family lines, it's understandable if one wants to know where they are and what they're doing now. Iceland today apparently takes pride in all of them—us—resident or not. That's why the government has sent out registration forms, trying to reach all the immigrants and families of immigrants in order to keep their records.[1] We're like those Daffodils in Kurt Vonnegut's book: we like to be counted in.

I told you that all Icelanders, both in Iceland and outside, can trace their ancestry to those disastrous, decimating times of the two plagues. The relative ease with which an Icelander can identify an ancestor may afford more than the personal satisfaction of tracing a family tree. Recently geneticists have begun to be aware of enormous potential in the homogeneity of

---

1 You will find such a registration form at http://www.iceland.org/regist2.htm. Keep in touch!

Icelanders.[2] I know you'll be interested in this, Kate, because you work for a pharmaceutical company.

"If you choose two Icelanders in the twentieth century," says Hákon Guðbjartson, chief computer engineer for a new company investigating genetics, "it's very likely they are distantly related. If you go back to the 15th century, you can more or less connect everybody to the same ancestors."

The culling of the population by bubonic plague in the 15th century and the volcanic eruptions in the 18th, combined with the Icelandic national lust for lists and records, has resulted in a project which will have a profound effect on the world's knowledge of genetically transmitted diseases recurrent within families. Icelandic-born Kári Stefánsson, a former Harvard Medical School professor, specializing in human genetics, has founded a company, Decode Genetics, Inc. and set up a research lab in order to search out the genes that are believed to cause 12 of the most prevalent diseases, such as multiple sclerosis; psoriasis; preeclampsia (characterized by high blood pressure during pregnancy); family tremors (uncontrollable trembling in the elderly); and breast cancer.

Michael Specter followed up this breaking story with an in-depth piece in *The New Yorker* (January 18, 1999) about the principals involved. As a prime example of the exciting nature of the news, he cited a major discovery by the Icelandic Cancer Society of the only breast-cancer mutation in Iceland, completely traceable to a 16th-century cleric named Einar. The first step to finding a cure is to be able to isolate the cause.

Kári Stefánsson has signed a multimillion-dollar contract with the Swiss drug company Hoffman-La Roche. Both participants think the deal will be worth two to three hundred

---

2 Most of this information is taken from the October 23, 1998 issue of the Icelandic weekly newspaper, *Logberg-Heimskringla,* from an article published originally in the *Los Angeles Times*, written by Mary Williams Walsh, and reprinted by permission.

million dollars, plus royalties, within the next five years. Kári believes that Iceland is a natural genetic hunting ground because of its geographic isolation, disasters, disease and ingrown breeding. The information the hunt yields will lead to a new industry; the identification and then the development of treatment for a variety of hereditary diseases. I might note in passing that one other place has also been receiving this kind of personal attention: Newfoundland, and for much the same reasons. It's isolated, insular, with a fairly clear and undiluted genetic stream.

I don't consider this genetic purity an argument for inbreeding. On the contrary, outside marriages strengthen a genetic line, bringing in new blood and diluting any weaknesses in the original DNA. One has only to look at the infamous royal families of ancient Egypt, or the Incans, to be reminded of what too much close intermarriage can do to the descendents. Besides, too much intermarriage can make you look like your cousin's sister. Do you remember that absurd riddle?

What is the difference between a duck?

One of its legs is both the same.

That's what happens in closed societies like Iceland and Newfoundland; people start to look like each other because they're so closely related. In Iceland, less than 1 percent of the population comes from anywhere else, mainly from the other Scandinavian countries, with just that one influx from Vietnam in the 1970s.

So it's understandable that the Icelandic database will be a research analyst's dream, comprising Iceland's impeccable collection of medical records dating from 1915 on; plus DNA samples of innumerable Icelandic donors; plus invaluable information locked in tissue samples, preserved in wax blocks, of every Icelander who has had an autopsy since the 1930s. Add to that church records: complete birth, baptism, marriage and death registries going back to Roman Catholic times, shortly after Iceland was declared Christian in AD 1000, and working forward through the Protestant Reformation when the national religion became Lutheran. Modern-day information, including census statistics and the national obsession with genealogy, brings the data to fulsome proportions. Once fed into computers, this information will simplify the task of discovering the through-lines of disease-causing genes, set as they will be against a uniform background, making recognition of deviations easier. Icelanders with lengthy family trees (they *all* have lengthy family trees!), and with a long history of hereditary disease, will be asked for current blood samples, for both the healthy and sick family members. All the people have to do is surrender their family trees and some DNA samples.

Understandably, not everyone is thrilled with the idea. The project is considered an invasion of privacy by some families, who have refused to be investigated. The benefits would seem to outweigh the disadvantages, one of the biggest benefits being that if the project results in the discovery of any new treatments, they will be given to Icelanders free of charge.

This discussion is a long way from a consideration of our little family tree, Kate. Does it mean anything to you? Perhaps not. Like any mother, you would simply reduce the family ailments to a personal level. Cousin Margrét used to comment that our children and grandchildren are bound to get either the Tergesen ulcers or the Tergesen arthritis. (What about the Tergesen osteoporosis? Something for you to look forward to?) It could be worse. Your brother is concerned that his father and his father's brother and his father's father died of heart attacks. My own father survived his heart attack to die of cancer 10 years later. I keep pointing out our Viking ancestry—those men died of rot, finally shuffling off in their nineties, most of them, in spite of cancer and God knows what all.[3] None, to my knowledge, was shot by a jealous husband.

Family members who know their own background may be able to arm themselves against future troubles if they pay heed in time. You know I keep telling you to pay close attention to me when I complain, because you could end up with the same ailment. The bonus in your genes is the tremendous vitality and life force of Icelanders. All our ancestors, having survived so much, had to withstand even more: inadequate food and so few greens that scurvy became almost a national epidemic. In her prize-winning novel, *The Prowler*, Kristjana Gunnars refers to leprosy among Icelanders, which surprised me. I thought the disease occurred only in hot countries: Bible lands, India, Hawaii. Not so. Iceland had lepers. And yet people survived. The tough bodies who lived to tell the tales could weather, it seemed, anything, even Manitoba winters. I guess there's something to be said for plain living and high thinking.

Some thinking wasn't all that high, though. You won't have had time to read the sagas yet, darling, but let me tell you how vicious and bloodthirsty the Vikings were, and not only the Vikings. After the Alþing was established (A.D. 930), the men and women of the country gathered annually to air their complaints and ask for judgement on their affairs. Judgement might be passed down and a fair allotment for redress of grievances given, but, although there was a judicial body, there was no executive side, no law enforcement. It was up to the plaintiffs to rally their own forces, their kinsmen and allies, to mete out the punishment and recover their land, chattels and pride, whatever was at stake. Overkill happened all too often and then resentment and blood feuds proliferated from generation to generation. Needless to say, a lot of blood was shed.

---

3 It's very pleasant to count on one's ancestors for some things; my lack of seasickness, for example. Whether we were Vikings or fishermen way back, we had to have some familiarity with the sea.

Perhaps that, too, culled the populations. Consider this: maybe all the bloodthirsty fighters were killed, leaving a nation of peacemakers, mild-mannered people. I'll tell you, Kate, I have never heard an Icelandic man raise his voice, let alone seen one raise his fist. Iceland does not have an armed military force. The 1992 census reported 2,200 active NATO-sponsored duty personnel, divided 80:20 between navy and air force, no army at all. The United States continues to operate the air base it established at Keflavik during the Second World War, with greatly reduced numbers. Military expenditures in Iceland account for zero percent of the GNP. I like that.

When I was touring Iceland by bus with other tourists on my first trip there, we were all in the middle of nowhere (most of the time!) and needed a pit stop. The driver remembered a church that was fairly close, assuring us that it would be open and we could use the facilities. While I was waiting my turn I peeked inside the sanctuary and saw that the communion pieces were on display on the altar. I went to take a look. There, in an empty, unlocked church, were a beautiful flat salver and a large pitcher, both of exquisite modern design and both made of sterling silver. So when I was told that there was very little significant crime, that is, homicide, in the country, I was ready to believe it. According to some stories I have heard, the police force is almost as idle as the Maytag repair man and spends a lot of time playing cards, on call but seldom in action. I have no proof, though. I do know they don't carry guns.

When he was there in 1935, Auden noticed that lost wallets were instantly returned to their owners, strangers or not. In Canada, that kind of honesty makes the news. It must be nice to live in a place where you not only know who your neighbour is, you trust him. Scientists tell us that depression can be inherited (blue genes?). Maybe honesty can, too.

—LOVE, MOM

CHAPTER FIVE

NORDIC WOMEN
—LETTER TO MY GRANDDAUGHTERS

DEAR JANICE, MEG, JENNIFER, PAIGE AND EMILY:
You're all pretty diluted Icelanders by this time, with so many other genes in your DNA, but you all have this in common: you call me Amma. And do you remember, Janice, when I returned from Iceland after my first visit and explained that Icelandic has more specific terms for family relationships? I told you that your uncle John, your mother's brother, was *moður broður*, literally, mother's brother; since then you have called him Mobro.

Be that as it may, you are my granddaughters and it is fitting that I tell you something of your female heritage on the Viking side. Icelandic women over the centuries have been a strong presence, not merely popping up now and then in the sagas and romances, more often, of course, in the romances. They were prized from the earliest Viking times in a land that was short of people; grown women were prized, that is, not infant girls. Too many girls meant too many mouths to feed; better to expose them—leave them to the elements—no less humane than garbage cans or dumpsters in the 20th century, but with slightly more reason. Once adult and able to bear children, a woman who was not barren was worth her weight in hired hands, being able to produce between 16 and 25 babies in her fertile years, averaging out around 10 or 12. Mind you, only two or three of those babies might live to useful adulthood. A lot of things could happen to an infant in those lean, primitive times, and did, no matter how much their mothers cared for them. Premature death just happened, it was to be expected. Still, the proven ability to bring forth a live child or two gave a woman a certain amount of power; she could divorce an unworthy husband knowing that she could easily find another who would be eager to impregnate her.

A woman's real economic worth, however, lay in her skill with a spindle. The tool is as powerful a metaphor as the sword is for a man; both were weapons in the battle for survival. The three Fates of Norse mythology were spinners and weavers. The Norns—Urda (the Past), Verdandi (the Present) and Skuld (the Future)—were women, spinning out people's lives. The most powerful goddess Freya was said to be a superb spinner; her greatest gift to a human woman was tireless, dazzling skill. While Iceland's chief farming product had been hay for its flocks of sheep, its chief export, and the clearest unit of value—until the value of fish was realized about the end of the 14th century—was the homespun cloth produced by the spinning and weaving women of the country.[1] This gave women power as well as respect; they were a full working partners in the household enterprise. From earliest times there was either a special, separate hut or a special room added to the hall *(baðstofa)* where the weaving was produced and where men were not allowed entrance. Only the god Oðin, once, it was reported, was granted audience in Freya's weaving room, where he learned female magic *(seiðr)*. Our foremothers, then, were competent in their production of cloth and babies.

Much of a family's economy depended on the product of the women's skill, not only their own clothes, but marketable commodities. Men could and did knit, but generally it was the women who did not only the knitting but also the

---

1 Information taken from an article, "The Role of Icelandic Women in the Sagas and in the Production of Homespun Cloth," by Nanna Damsholt, in the *Scandinavian Journal of History* 19 (1984).

more valuable spinning and weaving. Everyone, even the very youngest girls and boys, had production quotas to meet, every night, after the physical, outdoor work of the day was done. Tired as they might be, they still had to finish a certain number of yards or garments or whatever before they could go to sleep—a far cry from your lives, my darlings, when you beg to stay up to watch another television show.

A *wake-pick* was used to keep the knitters awake for work; it's "a device made from a small stick of wood with a slit on one side to catch the eyelid. It was used in old Iceland to keep the eyelids open when people had to stay up nights turning out the quota of knitting required to survive."[2] Kristjana Gunnars's book of poetry, *Wake-Pick Poems*,[3] is a collection of sequences ("Monkshood Poems," "Changeling Poems" and the title series), to do with folk superstitions, spells, herbal lore, myths and sexual terror— all very female. Don't forget the storytellers, who supplied *koldvaka* (cold wakefulness), another way to keep the workers going.

Halldór Laxness, in his Nobel-Prize-winning book, *Independent People*, describes the family's knitting and sewing industry at night. It was not merely a way of life, it was a means of it. Knitting turned out to be the means of survival in a different way in the New World. The Aboriginals who had to share the district of Keewatin (to the north of the little province of Manitoba) with the newly arrived Western Icelanders were impressed with the warmth of the socks and mitts the new settlers gave them—traded, rather. The Aboriginals had animal hides which were waterproof, but they welcomed the warmth and comfort of Icelandic knitting. The settlers traded mittens for fish. One story has it that an immigrant met a native man with

---

2 This description taken from the back cover of the book.
3 Toronto: Anansi, 1981.

bare hands on the trail one frigid winter day and peeled off one of the pairs of mitts he was wearing because he thought the poor man's hands must be freezing. He had a friend for life after that. Who would have thought that good knitting made good neighbours? It makes me wonder whether the West Coast Indians' skill for creating their famous Siwash sweaters was learned from the Western Icelanders.

For centuries Iceland was a hard hard place to live in, with a high mortality rate. As the *Poetic Edda* said, cattle die and kindred die, only the name of an honourable person lives on. It lived on in the hearts and minds and on the tongues of storytellers. For centuries, the names of people, both honourable and not, were preserved in stories told in the flickering light of lamps lit to aid the night work. This creation, as you will see, was a priceless commodity, more precious than jewels.

Think about it: the land had no precious stones or metals, no granite, no material with which to create soaring cathedrals, impregnable castles or precious artifacts. The people didn't even have the wherewithal to make music, lacking the wood or metal with which to fashion musical instruments. They had their voices and their minds. They had words and they had time—all the dark winter nights as they wove dreams and fabric and knitted up garments and the ravelled sleeve of care. As far as I can tell, the women were in this activity with the men; spinning stories was a joint enterprise.

The women carried it one step further: they were the first acknowledged teachers. In later centuries they gave the gift of literacy to their children. This, too, sprang from people's preoccupation with family, genealogy, bloodlines, names. How could a name live on without human memories to sustain it? How was it sustained without narrative, and eventually, finally, without writing it down? And then, how was it retrieved and perpetuated without reading? It was no accident that Icelanders were 100 percent literate from the mid-18th century on. Literacy was their most valuable tool and they made the most of it. Again, as far as I can tell, no distinction was made between male and female opportunities for literacy. If anything, the women might have been more skilled because they had more home time—not to be confused with leisure time—and also because they were the first educators of the children, both in the old world and the new. Early home schooling was another major contribution of Icelandic women to their culture, and this practice continued in New Iceland. A school was started during the very first year of settlement. According to its records, attendance was sparse; there were (never-ending) chores to be done elsewhere. However, the people remained literate, continuing to learn as they had been accustomed to do—at home, at night, by lamplight, at their mother's knee. Canada was obliging, too, offering plenty of long nights and a chilly incentive to stay indoors. Icelanders continued to be imbued with a love of language.

You may be pleased to learn, my darlings, that Icelandic women are very strong-minded, but you probably already knew that. They have been for centuries, beginning way back when they were won as spoils of victory and handed over with the goods and chattels to their Viking conquerors. If I can judge by the heroine Signy in *The Volsunga Saga*, the women often took their vengeance with as bloodthirsty a zeal as their menfolk, notwithstanding that they had borne their new lords' children. Later, when the Alþing was functioning, laws were passed in A.D. 1000 stating that a woman had equal rights in marriage. When she demanded a divorce from an unworthy husband, she was entitled to receive half her husband's possessions if she could prove her claim, and if she could enforce it. Just as a man, a woman was as strong as the family and friends who would support her.

There is full evidence in the sagas that women could command that kind of fealty. In *The Laxdaela Saga*,[4] a 15-year-old woman named Guðrun Ósvifsdóttir was married off by her father to a man called Þorvald who wooed her at the Alþing. Osvif settled the marriage contract which provided that Guðrun should manage her money affairs alone, and be entitled to one-half of the couple's property, no matter how long or briefly they were married. Þorvald was charged to buy her jewels to maintain her standards in the community, but without damaging the farm-stock with the cost of them. That would be considered a good settlement these days, except that Guðrun wasn't asked about her feelings, which she didn't like. So after her wedding to a man she didn't love, she cost her husband dearly with her extravagance, and in the meantime became very "friendly" with a man called Þord who was also married, to a woman called Aud. Finally, Þorvald had enough. She demanded another gift and he said she showed no moderation and boxed her ear.

Then Guðrun said, "Now you have given me that which we women set great store by having to perfection—a fine colour in the cheeks—and thereby have also taught me how to leave off importuning you." And she separated from him that spring and went home.

Guðrun and Þord rode together to the next Alþing, where Þord declared his separation from Aud, standing at the law rock and naming witnesses. Needless to say, Aud's brothers didn't think much of this, and there were repercussions. If you're interested, you can read the whole story for yourselves.

I went into a little detail to show you that although young Guðrun was forced into marriage by her father, she was given a handsome marriage settlement and she enjoyed

---

4 I'm condensing the story and quoting Guðrun from the translation of *The Laxdaela Saga*, available on the Internet as public domain. The URL is http://sunsite.berkeley.edu/OAMCL/Laxdaela/(chapter numbers here).html

great freedom. She had the right to end her marriage. Aud, you will be interested to know, took her own vengeance on Þord without waiting for her brothers to defend her honour.

There is a theory of invention that says we all stand on the shoulders of giants, that originality is incremental, proceeding from the immediately preceding idea or discovery. Occasionally a genius makes a frog leap two or three jumps above the previous one, or perhaps takes a lateral step. Usually, however, without the first there is no next; without the one, there is no other to follow. And so it is with those women; without them I, you, we, wouldn't be where we are today. Gracious men admit it, generously. Here's a tribute to women taken from an editorial in *Framfari*, the first Icelandic newspaper published in New Iceland:

> In accordance with all human experience it is ever the case that men make little progress along the way unless the women come to their assistance. It is from his mother that a child usually receives his first education, and it is always youthful influences which fasten the deepest roots in the heart and are the last to be discarded. In their mature years there is always the risk that men will try to employ force and vehemence in order to have their way, but then the womenfolk come with their gentle calm, their placid manners, and accomplish in peace and quiet, with politeness, care and courtesy what vehemence alone could never accomplish.

I want to say a word to you about witches before I settle too firmly in the New World. Like the rest of Europe, Iceland had its witches and its witch hunts, also known in Europe during the Inquisition and the Reformation. After the infamous witch-hunting manual *Malleus Maleficarum (The Magic Hammer)* burned its way across Europe, singeing Copenhagen in 1489 and spreading to Iceland, this unique manifestation of human belief was dubbed

Galdrabrennuöld—The Age of Wizards—unique indeed in Iceland because, according to historian Nelson Gerrard,[5] most of those convicted and burned were men. The "burning times," encouraged by burning laws in Denmark (never officially legislated in Iceland), characterized a certain fanatical fervour during the 17th century, during which some 22 wizards and one witch were burned at the stake in Iceland. Perhaps so few people were burned because wood was so scarce! The fact is, if fact can be associated with witchcraft, that superstition played a huge role in the formation of the Icelandic psyche; women with the skills of sorcery as well as second sight *(skyggni)* were generally heeded, if not honoured.

I've already mentioned their equal treatment at the Alþing, which dates from A.D. 1000. History tells us that the poet Snorri Sturluson, who lived in the 13th century, married a rich widow; this tells me that women held property in their own right. These and other evidences in the sagas indicate that Icelandic women were accorded great freedom and respect, enjoying full property and voting right from early times. They expected the same treatment in New Iceland.

The suffrage movement in Canada began in the late 1880s and Icelandic women in Manitoba were among its first leaders. Margrét Benedictsson (no record of her patronymic) was born in Iceland, in 1866, and on her own by the time she was 13. She emigrated to North Dakota in 1887 and moved to Winnipeg, where she married Sigfús Benedictsson in 1892. Her husband set up a printing press in Selkirk in 1898 and the couple began to publish *Freyja*, "the only woman suffrage paper published in Canada."[6] Margrét was the editor of this 40-page monthly magazine, a literary journal as well as a woman-suffrage polemic. *Freyja* thrived from 1898 to 1910, when Margrét's

5 *The Icelandic Heritage,* Arborg, Manitoba: Saga Publications & Research, 1986.

failing eyesight forced her to give it up. However, she continued the campaign for women's rights through the
formation of local suffrage societies (Winnipeg, Gimli, Shoal
Lake) and public speaking. By 1912 the well-known writer
and suffragist Nellie McClung added her powerful support,
and in 1914 headed a delegation to Sir Rodmond Roblin,
then premier of the province of Manitoba, at which the
Icelandic Women's Suffrage Association was represented.

The First World War both hindered and helped the
cause—delayed, I should say, rather than hindered. Women
put aside their own concerns in order to help in the war
effort. That help was so magnificent that most provincial
governments expressed their appreciation by granting
women the franchise. Manitoba was the first province to do
so, in 1916. It should be noted that the third reading of
the bill was moved by Acting Premier T. H. Johnson, himself the son of an Icelandic suffrage pioneer.

An Icelandic woman has always been her own self.
Today in Iceland she keeps her patronymic past marriage
and is known, as are the men, by her first name. Now I
want to tell you about Vigdis, who is a modern, international role model, the thinking woman's *Fjallkona*, listed as
one of the hundred most influential women in the world
today. Four times elected president of the republic of
Iceland, she is a national icon and a travelling promotion
tool. In January 1998, UNESCO named her chairperson of
the World Committee on the Ethics of Scientific Knowledge
and Technology. This, after she "retired" from public life.
One of her last official duties as president was the opening
of the Emigration Museum at Hofsos. She is as lovely up
close as she is in her pictures.

It has been said that young Icelandic women look like
Barbie® dolls, and there's some truth in the image: blue

---

6 Sigfús Benedictsson, from a private letter written August 5, 1946, quoted in *The
Icelandic People in Manitoba*, by Wilhelm Kristjanson, Winnipeg: R.W.
Kristjanson, 1965.

eyes, blond hair, with high, round cheekbones and breasts, as lithe and slim as whippets. But don't forget, girls, that Icelandic women are strong, also reticent, funny, stubborn, and powerful. Aren't these wonderful adjectives? Especially when they're apt and accurate. Well, from Barbie dolls to power! I have a favourite line from the much-quoted *Hávamál*, the poetic aphorisms in the *Elder Edda,* which are the Icelandic equivalent of the sayings of Confucius. I must say that it's nice to have the truth about women corroborated from such a respectable source. "Men's minds," the line goes, "are unstable towards women." You know that, don't you? Or if you don't, you'll soon find out. As you may surmise, I am more concerned with Icelandic women's minds and hearts than with their appearance.

The *Elder Edda* states, "The mind knows only what lies near the heart." These words are the theme of my play *Veranda*, the one I set on the veranda of my grandparents' home in Gimli, Manitoba, and which was loosely based on their lives as immigrants, plus stories I had heard and some I made up. Several characters use those words of the *Elder Edda* to underscore their behaviour. Although I give the chief interest in Norse literature to two of the men—father and son—I have given the truth of the words to two of the women, mother and daughter. Their honesty with themselves and with others is the backbone of my play. There is no compromise with truth, hard as it may be to acknowledge or live by. *Veranda* is really about the women, especially the woman—Anna, the matriarch.

The Norse outlook allows for no compromise. It's simple and understated and harsh. One could break one's knees or one's heart on it. Nothing in northern life leads one to expect anything else. Fate and the weather play for keeps. I believe that climate and terrain contribute to the building—or the destruction—of a soul. The uses of adversity are hard to recognize and if one had a choice, one would rather do without that kind of character scouring. Still, it's bred in the bone after living with it for a few generations. A soft wind and a mild temperature can create a trust in weather that no northern-bred character shares. Cold is still a killer, and not to be trusted. Even today with climate-controlled houses and cars, people—drunk or careless—can go too far into a sub-zero night and gently die of the cold. To lie down in such weather without a struggle is to die. A cousin of mine (your first cousin, once removed) did just that, in Gimli. He froze to death one night when he inadvertently locked himself out of the house. Even struggle does not guarantee life. The odds are high and harsh.

Northern people have always been aware of the odds. We find them acknowledged in the earliest writings, in Norse literature and in *Beowulf* and the other earliest extant poetry in Anglo-Saxon. In *The Seafarer*, snow, "coldest of corn," is sown as seeds of struggle and reaps a harvest of cold and suffering; *The Wanderer*, too, tells of a cold exile far from home and hearth.

I know these are essentially masculine narratives, describing the journey and the struggle out in the cold world. Women tend that warm hearth and wait at home for their cold seafarers and wanderers. What do they know of the cold that puts steel into men's souls and of the endless struggle with the elements and with Fate? They see their men struggle and endure and lose but never compromise. They know, as the men do, that there are no guarantees, no soft landings or happy endings. The important thing is to endure. A hero might die but he never *says* die. Is that solely a masculine prerogative?

You must surely know, my darlings, that as a woman I will deny that it is, and that as a woman writer I will write about women who display the same kind of heroism and endurance as their menfolk. Not for them the external physical hardships or the tangible dragon, though they certainly may suffer physically, in childbirth, for example, inexorably and continually in other centuries before this one when they had no choice. They often endure a greater psychic pain because their struggles are internal, not to be vented or released in physical confrontation. I maintain that Northern women display the same heroic traits inspired, perhaps, by the sagas and tempered by the climate: tough qualities of honesty, courage and endurance, coupled with a pragmatic spirit that enables them to accept the inevitable.

You can read stories of pioneer women in the history of North America, Icelandic women among them. I'm not going to repeat them, though they are inspiring and well worth reading. I am a writer, as you know, so I have created some female characters who embody a number of the qualities I have observed in Nordic women. What qualities? you ask. First of all is the ability to keep living each day as if it mattered.

"Life is so daily," says Anna in my play *Mark*, "why can't I get used to it?"

"You?" says her husband, Mark, who is dying of cancer. "You're the one who teaches us all about present time."

Anna insists on taking Mark's ebbing life day by day and refuses to contemplate her future without him. At the same time, some stubborn pragmatic streak impels her to send his funeral suit to the cleaners—the one he will wear in his coffin—and to muse aloud that he won't be needing his winter coat. It's so tactlessly matter-of-fact, it makes the audience laugh.

"We go day by day, and you can't allow yourself to think about tomorrow, or next week, or next year," says Peggy Woodgreen in my play *A Place on Earth,* the story of an old woman alone in her room with only a puppet for company. It is my most popular play because there are lonely old women in rooms all over the world.

Bravery is not an adjective usually ascribed to women. Seventy-two-year-old Peggy Woodgreen knows that too. "How often does a woman my age get to be brave?" she asks her daughter in a telephone conversation, and on hearing her daughter's reply, is touched:

"Why, what a nice thing to say! Do you really think I'm brave every day?"

She is. Women are. They don't fight dragons, they fight the dailies, and they brace themselves for the crises. I think bravery is an attitude of mind, not a performance.

"The mind knows only what lies near the heart." If you get too far away from the heart, you're in danger of not knowing what you mean. Women stay close to the heart and keep a clear eye.

"When I was a girl," says Anna in *Veranda*, "I never wanted the rainbow. I wanted the Well of Knowledge because I am not very smart."

"You, Mama?" says her son Svenn, who has been spouting Norse mythology with drunken enthusiasm as she struggles to get him to bed. "You, Mama? You're smart."

"No," she says, "but I work hard to make up for it."

Women do—work hard. The labour was literal and continuous in the days before birth control. Women used to pray to die before their children, a wish that was not always granted. In *A Place on Earth*, Peggy Woodgreen, living in modern times, isn't spared that pain. Her only son died in a car crash in his late teens. Peggy has been a widow for 16 years and at 72 has lost many of the friends of her youth. In fact, she says, "It's getting so I know more people in the cemetery than on the street."

I think again of the *Edda:*

> *Cattle die and kindred die,*
> *We also die.*
> *But I know one thing that never dies,*
> *Judgement on each one dead.*

There's no turning back. Somehow I've always known that. I didn't learn it from the sagas, or maybe I did, if it has become part of my genetic structure. Anyway, I seem always to have known it. It has been bred into me. Peggy Woodgreen agrees, of course. How could she not? She's my character.

"Too late now," she says, so discouraged with her life but knowing she can't quit. "There's no turning back. The only way is through. Go through. Get on with it."

Endurance. Now we're getting to it, the dogged endurance of the Nordic spirit that I share with my characters. Peggy wants to kill herself. She tells her puppet, "I've told you, I can't stay here any longer. I can't, I can't stand it. Now—do it!" And she raises a butcher knife in her puppet's arms, begging him to kill her. But he/she doesn't. She has to keep on keeping on, and tries to make the best of it. I think it's the secret of happiness, one that few of us learn, not without a lot of practice. Or maybe it's the key to contentment, or maybe, simply, to acceptance.

"What's wrong with the women of this family?" Loa asks her mother, Karin, in *Veranda*. "Are we all doomed to unhappiness?"

"I don't notice the men dancing in the streets," says Karin. "We all do what we can, we live."

"I think," says Anna, their grandmother and mother respectively, "no matter what we do, there is pain. We do what we think is best, and then we live with what we choose."

The Danish philosopher Søren Kierkegaard defined freedom as "the consciousness of necessity." I think Nordic women recognize necessity. Does that make them free? They do what has to be done. Kate in *Mark* assists at her father's deathbed and helps him out of life, doing what has to be done. Women do that, my women with their Nordic common sense.

"Death is not easy to hide from," sings the poet-narrator in *Beowulf*. "The time will come for every man when his loan of days is done." For every woman too. Her loan of days will be done too.

"Þaes ofereode," says the poet in the Anglo-Saxon poem, *Deor's Lament. "Þaes ofereode; þises swa maeg." That passed; so may this*. Until it does, we have to endure.

That is the implicit lesson of the sagas, and it's the lesson Icelandic women have learned well. Their souls have inhaled it with every breath of northern air. They don't have to like it, but they'll endure it.

"You *are* going to live," says Peggy Woodgreen, after failing to commit suicide, "make no mistake about that. You're going to live and you're going to keep on living until you are permitted to die... I won't go barnstorming the gates of eternity again. I'll wait 'til I'm invited."

Sometimes it takes a long time to be invited. Icelandic women are the longest-lived women in the world, and Western Icelandic women aren't far behind. According to the most recent statistics from Iceland, the life expectancy of a girl child born today is 81.21 years, about half a year ahead of North American women. But if you were to read the birthday news in the Icelandic Canadian newspaper, *Logberg-Heimskringla*, it seems there's scarcely a week goes by that an old woman in Betel, the senior citizens' home in Gimli, isn't celebrating her hundred-and-somethingth birthday. The fact is, we're here to stay a while. After all, we've stuck it out this long. Why?

It's a mindset, a climate of the soul, and I think it is shared by people who live in northern latitudes, engendered in part by harsh weather and Spartan living conditions that test the mettle of a human being. Not that we in Canada are very Spartan any more, nor are they in Iceland. But for all those centuries past Icelanders did not have enough to eat. Icelanders have starved to death, suffered tuberculosis and leprosy, and been politically and economically oppressed, first by Norway, then by Denmark. Even today, with enough (expensive, imported) food, Iceland is still not the easiest place to live, especially if a person suffers from SAD (Seasonal Affective Disorder), a syndrome that afflicts people who miss light during the dark months of winter. Still, I think I discovered the secret of its inner light and also the secret of its comfort. These are part of what has made Icelanders strong.

What I have to consider now is how all this touches me as a Western Icelander. Your grandmother, girls (me), is solid Canadian on my father's side, from United Empire Loyalist stock. That had to have some effect. And of course, I acknowledge that what I experienced of things Icelandic was at two or three removes. But there are other women as "removed" as I am to whom this connection is just as important.

I met Katrina (to whom I addressed my letter on Kinship) at a Thorrablót (an Icelandic feast) put on by the Icelandic Canadian Club in Toronto. She is a third-generation Western Icelander; her great-grandfather was only three years old, the youngest of 10 children, when he arrived in New Iceland; her grandparents were born here. Katrina has been gathering the story of her *amma* and *afi,* who slugged out a hard existence on the land. Compiling memories of her kin and weaving these in with what her *amma* told her, she has created a moving story that expresses in its essence the saga of the New Icelanders. I asked her permission to quote from her book, *Íslensk Kona,* not yet published. Her *amma's* words express, I think, this dual vision that we share:

> As the years went by, I would come to understand that my family's Icelandic stories and melodies were an important part of who I was. I would grow to learn a deep respect for

heritage and to gain the belief that my family's roots, stretching over prairies, and far across the sea, was something to be proud of. I would honour my family's commitment to our cultural roots by growing up confident in my identity as both a Canadian and an Icelander. No matter what life had in store for me I would always know who I was.

In *Veranda*, the daughter of the immigrants has been invited to be *fjallkona* (Maid of the Mountain) at Íslendingadagurinn (Icelandic Celebration Day), and she dutifully asks her father's permission. In my story, the character has for years resented his refusal to let her marry before her soldier went to serve in the First World War. He did return to her but died young and she blames her father for the lost years. When her father gives Karin permission to be *fjallkona*, he asks her to find it in her heart to forgive him. In Gimli, the Maid is no maid but a mature woman who has contributed to the community for years. So this speech I wrote for my *fjallkona* is that of a mature woman looking back on her youth, trying to understand her life and her connection with the past. That's what I'm trying to do, too.

My dear friends, today you have honoured me and my family more deeply than I can say. It is a great privilege for me to stand before you as your Maid of the Mountain for 1950 and speak to you as compatriot, neighbour, and friend. Those of you who know me well will have trouble relating my present dignity to the agony of the little girl who slid down the old wooden slide, the fire escape on Gimli Public School, and got a bottom full of slivers. My father had to carry me home and my mother picked out all the slivers while my father told me stories from the sagas until he was hoarse to keep my mind occupied with other things. He never reminded me that I had been forbidden to play on the slide. Instead, he told me about Egill, who taunted the gods and risked his life and won reprieve with his art. I had forgotten about the slivers and about Egill until just recently when I began to read the sagas for myself, in preparation for this day.

And then there was the time I went horseback riding, also against orders, on a skittish horse that ran away with me. I stayed on, but my ankles were lacerated and bloody because I wore no boots and the stirrups cut into my flesh. Again my father carried me home—a good deal heavier by this time—and poured me a brandy while Mama washed away the dirt and the tears and waited for the doctor to come. My first brandy it was—what a shocking thing for a Maid of the Mountain to confess that she began drinking at the tender age of eleven! It eased the pain, as I remember, and I did not become a drunkard. In fact, I believe, with the writer of the Elder Edda, that

There lies less good than most believe

In ale for mortal men

—and for mortal women, too. Later, when I was older, at least seventeen, some friends and I were stranded by a sudden storm—everyone here knows how sudden and treacherous the storms on Lake Winnipeg are—and it was my father who found us the next morning, beached on the far side of Hecla Island, safe, but cold and hungry. The other parents, I learned later, scolded their children—though we were not children, as they very well knew—and questioned them fearfully as to their behaviour overnight. My father never questioned me. He trusted me, always. As the wise man said, and this is the creed of all of us, is it not,

Thou knowest that I will not lie.

Never shalt thou be stained by baseness.

It was my father and my mother who taught me to speak Icelandic as I speak it to you now, and who made me learn to read it and write it, much against my will, for it was extra homework I didn't want when I was a girl. But I am grateful for it now. It was my father and my dear older brother Svenn—may his poor soul rest in peace—who taught me to love the Icelandic sagas and to realize that we are all of us, each in our way, still living out a saga in a new land in the twentieth century. It was my father and my mother who instilled in me the reverence for our past, the will to endure against all odds, and the serenity to accept what life offers us and to go on. I have not always been serene, I admit to you, but I have ever had the example of my father and mother before me to teach me this lesson.

When I go with you to lay the wreath on the cairn, it will be with humility and gratitude for the courage, and love, and wisdom of our ancestors—and of my father and mother. My prayer for us all is that we may continue to perform great deeds for our adopted or first-born country, Canada, and for our fathers and mothers who give us our enabling heritage.

The mind knows only
What lies near the heart.

I couldn't have said it better myself.

—LOVE, AMMA

CHAPTER SIX

FOOD
—LETTER TO MY GRANDMOTHER

DEAR AMMA:

The French chef Georges Auguste Escoffier (1846-1935) once said, "Tell me what you eat and I'll tell you what you are." I wonder what he would have said about people who eat rotted shark; air-hardened fish bodies, bones and all; rafter-hung, smoke-imbued mutton; and curdled milk. Mind you, he was not above eating black fungi dug up from the roots of trees by snuffling pigs, mouldy blue cheese and fermented grapes. People eat whatever food is available and pray that it is available. Only in the 20th century, only in the latter few decades of the 20th century, and only in an affluent society, can people choose to eat whatever delicacy they please from whatever land they please in whatever month they please. I wonder what becomes of feasts when feasts become commonplace? That's another discussion. I want to tell you, Amma, about my romance with Icelandic food—romance, that's right.

Do you remember Thorrablót? Jokingly, ever since I have been attending Thorrablót in Toronto for the past few years, I call it an Icelandic pig-out. That's exactly what it is, a feast to celebrate the month of Thorri, one of the months in the old Icelandic calendar, except that in Iceland the feasting on traditional food lasts for a month. The first day of Thorri corresponds to January 22 in the international calendar, a harsh, cold time of year in the northern hemisphere when one needs the strength of Thor to endure it.

A Western Icelander, several generations removed, would think it required the strength of Thor to eat the food! *Blót,* I was told, means sacrifice (blood), so the feast is a sacrifice to Thorri. Some people think Thorri was a different, lesser god than Thor, but my informant, Guðrun Guðsteinsdóttir, a professor at the University of Reykjavik, tells me that they're one and the same. She says that after Iceland was declared Christian, the bishops did their best to either eliminate or Christianize the reminders of the old Nordic religion. Thus, the ritual sacrifices to Thor and the month dedicated to him were disguised by using the diminutive Thorri, which doesn't sound as threatening.

Traditional delicacies at this time include pickled and sour sheep products, including singed sheep-heads *(svið)* blood and liver sausage *(slátur* and *lifrapylsa),* dried fish *(harðfiskur),* cured (rotted) shark *(hákarl),* and rams' testicles *(hrutspungar)*—in sausages. Until recently one of the specialities was singed sheep's feet pickled in whey *(surar sviðalappir).* What makes it possible to get all this food down is *Brennivin*—"Black Death." This has nothing to do with the 14th-century bubonic plague, it's a killer drink made of distilled potatoes and caraway seed, the Icelandic version of schnapps. Like vodka, it is traditionally drunk straight and is best served direct from the freezer. Some people like to serve it in a block of ice. I imagine if your tongue is partially paralyzed with alcohol and cold, it helps to make the *svið* go down.

My friend Guðrun, the source of all this information, says that people eat their festive food *(þorramatur* or Thorri-fare) for the whole month of Thorri. Apparently one can buy prepared trays with samplings of the different delicacies for lunch or supper. She says all the daycare centres serve the kids traditional food during Thorri, thus ensuring that future generations will develop similar, distinctive tastes. The best-seller, she says, that disappears first from the stores, is the pickled sausages made from rams' testicles. A January (Thorri) newspaper, Guðrun said, reported that the consumption of the treat is one and a half testicles per capita. I guess that figures, seeing as it is the virile Thor's month. I can just hear you giggling, Amma. I know you didn't eat anything like that in North America. The wonder is that they still do in Iceland. I mean, take the ram out of the flock and where are ewe?

People eat what's available, and what can be preserved—by smoking, salting, pickling, drying, and so on. For Icelanders, as for other people when on the brink of starvation, when food wasn't available, they even ate grass, tender, green, spring shoots, but grass all the same. Even with all the hardships the Western Icelanders suffered in the New World, I think they were probably better off food-wise almost from the first—almost. I know there were some lean years. But the feasting started early on, so they must have had something to celebrate, and something to celebrate with.

My friend Guðrun says that because of its association with the old religion, Thorrablót had been discontinued but was revived in Iceland around the turn of the century. The first one in Manitoba was held in Winnipeg on January 24, 1894, but the idea of it as an annual celebration didn't take hold until the 1950s, as near as my cousins and I can make out. Now it is celebrated all over North America, wherever there is an Icelandic or a Scandinavian Club, a little later in the year than Iceland, usually some time in March, although the month of Thorri ends on February 21 in Iceland. The food, as one might expect, is slightly different: no rams' testicles, no rotted shark, seldom *hangikjöt* (smoked lamb), unless it is imported. However, other exotic, distinctively Icelandic delicacies are available, and prized. At the Thorrablót I regularly attend, held by the Icelandic Canadian Club of Toronto, the "big meat" is roast turkey, which strikes me as very North American.

Your cooking, Amma, begun officially when you became a wife in the New World, had to be influenced by the ingredients of the New World. It was good, though, so good that in 1963 I made my first professional, big-time, writing sale ($200 U.S. from *Gourmet* magazine) for an article about your Icelandic cooking—Icelandic once removed, from Iceland to Gimli. Like people, food has to adapt to new surroundings. People take the tastes, the memories, habits and cooking methods, and apply them to whatever similar material they can find in the new locale. You did amazing things to Canadian-produced raw ingredients, but I didn't know that then. Even with the open mind of a child, albeit a child with a foot in two worlds, I had trouble adapting to some of the taste sensations I was introduced to during my summers in Gimli.

Mysostur (whey cheese) was a disappointment at first because it looked, but didn't taste, like peanut butter. *Skyr* (Icelandic yogurt) looked like thick cream but tasted sour to me. For some reason, I loved *hardfiskur* (hard or dried fish), probably because of all the butter I dug up to eat with it. Of course, I loved *vínar terta*; everyone does, after the surprise of the prune filling. I was told the word for this cake was in the new (1998) *Canadian Oxford Dictionary:* it's there, but spelled as one word. I've never seen it that way in the little Icelandic cookbooks that Icelandic clubs and church groups publish privately from time to time—the only Western Icelandic cookbooks that exist.

Am I being chauvinist when I say that Icelandic coffee is among the best in the world? Probably. Obviously, coffee beans are not indigenous to Iceland. Coffee wouldn't have reached Iceland until after it was brought back from the New World. Yet coffee is synonymous with Icelanders, with Western Icelanders, and by extension, with hospitality. Another thing synonymous with Icelanders is *molakaffi*, that is, coffee with a *molasykur*, a sugar cube in it. Not in it, exactly. It takes years to develop the skill of holding a sugar cube firmly between the teeth and drinking black coffee through it. I never got the hang of it. You'll remember that Afi was a whiz. I would be surprised, though, if the early settlers had sugar cubes. I have a vague memory of sugar in a huge block in Afi's store. I guess he chopped off his own lumps, like calves off a glacier.

The secret to good coffee, as you know, Amma, lies in the method—and, I would suggest, the water. Like the other Western Icelanders I observed, you made your coffee with a bag. Winnipeg wags called the Icelandic coffee bag a sock, but they didn't understand. It produced a filtered nectar at a time when people drank percolated coffee, which is an abomination. One of my earliest tasks as a little girl, related to my water-carrying, was to take the coffee bag to the well and wash it out. I remember the well in your backyard, just steps from the garden. Another one of my summer jobs was to gather the leaf lettuce for luncheon salad, and the carrots for dinner, and wash them in the flowing water. I think of the well and the coffee bag every morning now when I clean out the permanent coffee filter—better for the ecology of the planet than paper filters—of my Melitta® coffeemaker. I do it in cold running water, as I was taught.

One of my most cherished wedding gifts was a set of coffee bags from Auntie Anna. She made them out of unbleached sheeting and sewed the first one into a sieve handle with the mesh cut out, which fit into a quart-size enamel jug with a handle. Before being used, the bag had to be "seasoned," boiled in coffee until the fibres softened and picked up a little coffee oil for flavor. Each bag would last about two years and I fell into the habit of starting a new bag with each new baby, four of them, who arrived roughly two years apart. After that, I had to be more arbitrary and decide when to install a new bag. The sieve handle had to be replaced once in a while too, because it disintegrated.

One tablespoon of coffee went into the bag for each cup desired, along with a pinch of salt. Bubbly boiling water was poured over the coffee and it dripped into the pot, set on a low burner, replicating the heat at the back of a wood-burning stove. If the bag was new and too fast, the filtered coffee might have to be poured through a second time. I always transferred the coffee to a heated silverplate thermos jug so that it didn't have to be reheated. As a young homemaker, I was famous for my good coffee. The tap water in Winnipeg was pretty good but it must have been the method that made my coffee so special. I kept a silver trivet on the coffee table permanently. Every evening the jug went onto the trivet to supply my husband, Bill, and me with countless cups (demitasse, to cut down a little) of coffee until bedtime, which was always late. For years, before we discovered decaffeinated coffee, we thought everyone lay awake until after 2:00 a.m.! I am told that Afi never had this problem; coffee made him sleep, though no one can corroborate this now. I do know that decaf has a reverse effect on my brother and keeps him wide awake. I stopped making Icelandic coffee with a bag after Bill died. I didn't drink enough coffee by myself and the bag went dry between use and lost its savour, as did coffee time alone.

Coffee time in Gimli was a wonderful, twice-, even thrice-daily event: twice in the day and once every evening. Afi and my uncles walked home from the store for morning and afternoon coffee and gossip. Others joined the group: my mother and her sister, Auntie Anna, and assorted daughters-in-law and cousins, including a little girl who didn't care about the coffee but hoped for a slice of *vínar terta* or a piece of date bar (called matrimonial cake elsewhere in Canada). Sometimes there were other treats: *pönnukökur,* Icelandic pancakes rolled into tight cornucopias around brown sugar; or *kleinur,* deep-fried dough knots, dusted with icing sugar; and my favourite, but rare: *rosettes*, deep-fried butterfly or flower shapes loaded with strawberry jam and whipped cream.

Coffee time should have served as my first language lessons but everyone was too intent on delicious gossip to supply me with other than delicious food.

Coffee time in Iceland remains a special event. I don't know if coffee production still involves the use of a bag, probably not in restaurants or cafés. But the water is pure; in fact, Iceland is one of two places in the world where the boast is that you can put the water directly into a car radiator without damaging it. (The Highlands of Scotland is supposed to be the other place.) Good for the pipes is also good for the flavour. Anywhere I went in Iceland, the coffee was excellent, and exquisitely served. Even in a pit stop on the road, where the bus stopped to gas up and the tourists ran to the restrooms and the postcard counter, the coffee was served in a pretty cup on a saucer, rather than a disposable cup. One wet July afternoon in Akureyri, my companion and I stopped at a little restaurant for coffee and to get dry. As usual, a pretty cup and saucer arrived, this time on a service plate, with *lagniappe*: a little dish of two perfect chocolates, one each.

Mind you, it costs. Everything is pricey in Iceland and coffee is no exception. Beginning in the pit stops, it's $2.50 (CDN) a cup, and that was six years ago. You have to want it. I did.

I grew up and acquired adult tastes, including a taste for some of the Icelandic delicacies I ignored as a child. I have heard it said that ethnic food skips a generation. Frequently the first generation of an immigrant family wants desperately to conform to the customs of the New World and scorns the parents' traditions in dress, language, religion and food, among other things. If these children are successful as adults they may in time be more confident in acknowledging, even flaunting their background; it's colourful, it's different. All too often, however, the children of immigrants lose their distinctive characteristics in the blend of cultures encountered in their adopted country and become bland and uninteresting in an effort to conform. It takes the second generation, secure in the New World and curious about the old one, to start exploring the old ways. Food is one of the easiest areas for new/old discoveries. So it was with me and my mother.

Mother never made a *vínar terta* in her life. I had to get that recipe and others from her older sister, my Auntie Anna, the first child who had been old enough to carry on the old ways without question. I have to say in all fairness and in defence of my mother that her defection was the result of marrying outside the fold. Did you know that my father's two adoring, snobbish sisters thought he was such a "catch" in Winnipeg that they made life uncomfortable for your Inga when she was a brand-new, uncertain bride? She never complained, not to you, not to anyone, never told on them, only told me late in life, but she never recovered. She had no confidence in herself so how could she risk what little self-esteem she had by serving *fiskabollur?* Anyway, since my father was a lapsed Catholic, he hated fish in any form. So it remained to me to rediscover and reclaim family tastes, well and truly resurrected. I came home triumphantly from my second trip to Iceland with a wonderful recipe for *gravlax* from cousin Hebba, and made it in time to serve on New Year's Day when my son enjoyed it with me. He's been making it ever since. We both like it better than smoked salmon. As I say, it skips a generation, or two.

I notice that the word for salmon in Icelandic is *lax*. Did you know that the Yiddish word is *laks* (and North American slang makes it *lox*, but all of them are pronounced the same). Not only the sound and the spelling but also the taste sensation bear out part of my slightly facetious argument that the Icelanders are one of the lost tribes of Israel. There's a noticeable similarity between *gefilte* fish and *fiskabollur*. They're both best served with beets: beet horseradish or *chrain* with *gefilte* fish and boiled or pickled beets with *fiskabollur*. You think that's a weak argument, Amma? Think about it some more.

I doubt that you ever wrote down a recipe in your life. Somehow I inherited a piece of paper in my mother's handwriting which purported to be your recipe for *baunar supa* (bean soup). All it said was: "1 pound navy beans, 1 pound stew beef. Boil." From that I worked out one of my very best recipes that I used to serve at after-theatre parties when I did that sort of thing. I published that recipe in my article in *Gourmet* magazine and also in my first cookbook[1] but I'm going to include it here, along with some other foods, starting with

> *BAUNAR SUPA*
> *2 pounds white (navy) beans*
> *water*
> *1 tablespoon salt*
> *l large onion, quartered*
> *3 pounds stewing beef, cut in small pieces*
> *2 tablespoons butter*
> *2 bay leaves*
> *2 small onions, sliced*
> *1 bottle of beer*
> *1 cup small fresh mushrooms, sliced*
> *1 cup sour cream*
> *1 teaspoon dill seed, crushed*

First the beans: wash them well under cold, running water and then soak them overnight in enough cold

---

1 *Encore: The Leftovers Cookbook.* Toronto: McClelland & Stewart, 1975. Out of print.

water to cover. In the morning, rinse and drain them and add more cold water to cover, along with the salt and onion and boil gently until tender, about 1 1/2 hours or more. Beans vary. Test one every now and then by blowing on it. If the skin peels back under the pressure of your breath, the bean is cooked. Be sure to skim the froth from the surface of the liquid during the first half hour of cooking.

Now the meat: in a heavy Dutch oven or cast-iron saucepan with a lid, sear and brown the beef in the butter, add the bay leaves and the sliced onions, cover tightly and leave on low heat for an hour, or place it in a 325°F oven for one hour. Remove the bay leaves and add the cooked beans and bean liquor to the meat in the Dutch oven, stir gently to mix, and pour in the beer, adding more if there doesn't seem to be enough liquid.

In a separate pan, sauté the mushrooms until soft and golden. Stir in the sour cream and the dill seed (crushed in a mortar and pestle) and add this mixture to the soup, blending well. Cover and simmer the soup for two or three hours.

Serves 10, good for a party, with Icelandic brown bread and a green salad. It ripens wonderfully; if there's any left, it's even better the second day.

So now you want to see what's happened to Icelandic Brown Bread. My friend Katrina, whose Icelandic *amma* was born in Canada, gave me her family recipe for brown bread. It is delicious.

>*ICELANDIC BROWN BREAD*
>*1 tablespoon granulated sugar*
>*1/2 cup lukewarm water*
>*2 tablespoons dry yeast*
>*2 cups milk*
>*1/2 cup dark molasses*

1 tablespoon salt
2 tablespoons oil
1/2 cup brown sugar
6 cups whole wheat flour
4 cups white flour

Dissolve the granulated sugar in the lukewarm water and add the yeast, allowing it to bloom for about 10 minutes. Meanwhile, scald the milk, stir in the molasses, salt, oil, and brown sugar and allow to cool to lukewarm. Stir down the yeast, blend it into this mixture and stir it all into some of the flour in a large bowl. Beat well. Add the remainder of the flour as required. I usually spread the flour onto a board (or marble), dump the first mixture on top of it and go at it with my bare hands to mix and knead it thoroughly.

When you have a malleable, non-sticky mass, place it in a greased bowl, cover with waxed paper (in case it's still a little sticky) and a tea towel and let rise in a warm place till about doubled in bulk, for 1/2 hour to 45 minutes. If you're using the old-style yeast, punch the dough down and let rise again, another 1/2 hour. The new, single-rising yeast makes these two steps unnecessary, but I'm following the instructions according to Katrina's *amma*. Turn the dough back onto the board and cut it into four equal parts. Slap each section into a long, wide, thick rope and then fold it in on itself starting from one end, pushing it down with the heels of your hands as you roll it into a loaf form to squeeze out the air bubbles.

Shape and pat the loaf and put it in greased standard-size loaf pans. Put the four pans in a warm place, cover with a tea towel and let rise again, about 1/2 hour or until doubled in bulk. Preheat the oven to 400°F. Put the loaves into the oven and immediately turn down the heat to 325°F-350°F. Bake 45 to 60 minutes, until done. (When in doubt, you can ease a loaf out of the pan and tap the bottom with your fingers; if it sounds hollow, it's done.) Cool on wire racks. Makes 4 loaves.

I won't bother giving a recipe for green salad. Salads are very personal; everyone has her favourite combination of ingredients and preparation method, and you, Amma, were no exception. I still have a special fondness for your way of treating that tender leaf lettuce that I picked. The barely-torn leaves, sprinkled with a little white sugar and tossed in a tiny bit of white vinegar tasted sweet and full of sunshine.

W.H. Auden deplored Icelandic cooking and thought it very strange to sugar food, specifically, potatoes. I remember you used to stir grated nutmeg and a pinch or two of sugar into a white sauce to pour over boiled potatoes, and that was very good. In Iceland, they caramelize potatoes and serve them year round, but they are the traditional accompaniment to roasted *rjúpa* (ptarmigan) for Christmas dinner, or else *hangikjöt* (smoked lamb).

Icelandic potatoes are delicious, small and yellow, even more yellow than the popular Yukon Gold here. When I was last in Iceland, the potato crop had failed in parts of Europe, and Iceland was actually exporting some of its potatoes—amazing for a land so poor in produce. Let's hear it for greenhouses!

> *CARAMELIZED POTATOES[2]*
> *2 pounds small potatoes*
> *4 tablespoons butter*
> *1/3 cup white sugar*

Scrub the potatoes and boil whole until tender but firm,

---

2 Combining the methods from two sources: Icelandic National League (INL), *op. cit.*, and "Icelandic Recipes" found at http://www.iceland.org/matkjot.html.

peel them and transfer to a warmed bowl. (Save the potato water for the bread dough.) Brown the butter over low heat in the hot saucepan, stir in the sugar and turn up the heat, allowing the mixture to froth and brown. Lower the heat and quickly stir in the potatoes, rolling them in the mixture to coat them well until they are light brown. Return to the bowl and serve immediately or keep warm in a low oven.

You'll notice I'm not offering a recipe for pickled herring. As with green salads, the way people prepare their herring is a matter of extreme personal preference. However, I will mention pickled beets. There are, of course, elaborate ways to pickle and bottle beets to store for the winter. I don't do that. When I boil fresh beets to serve with fish, as you always did—such a lovely colour on the plate!—I deliberately cook too many. I slice the leftover beets, put them in a jar and cover them with apple cider vinegar. That's all. Next time I have fish, *fiskabollur* or *gefilte* fish, I have my pickled beets all ready. For extra pleasure, I drop a couple of tablespoons of horseradish on top of the beets when I serve them.

Amma, I will never forget your wonderful Sunday dinners. One of your most elegant main dishes was baked, stuffed whitefish—the big, beautiful whitefish Lake Winnipeg used to be famous for. I remembered it for a good purpose years later when a hunter-writer friend of ours in Winnipeg flew up to the Arctic Circle to catch, photograph and write about the northern fresh water fish, Arctic char, a plum assignment from *Sports Illustrated* magazine. I had never heard of Arctic char until Ralph came back with two of them and asked me to cook them (his English wife hated wildlife in any form and preferred to cook meat from the meat counter at her corner grocer's). I used your recipe. We had a dinner party and invited

Ralph and his wife and two other friends, Mary and Duff Roblin, who was then premier of the province of Manitoba.

It so happened that a week later, Duff was in Montreal at a premiers' conference and the chef at La Reine Elizabeth presented this august assembly with a new dish: Arctic char, which the government planned to release for retail sale the following week for the first time in Canada. Everyone was suitably impressed except Duff, who said, "That was very good, but I know a woman in Winnipeg who does it better!" Thanks to you, Amma.

I've never coped with a fish in its natural habitat in my life. I remember pedlars coming door to door in Gimli in the summer, selling fresh fish, and I guess that's where you bought yours, too. In those days I'm sure you had to scale and gut them. I don't.

I buy a nice, neat whole fish, all scaled and split and gutted, ready for me to cook. If I can, I buy the fish with the head on because the flesh will be moister when cooked and I know enough to wrap the head in foil to keep it together. But natural state? Uh uh. Anyone who wants to use my recipe had better know a reputable, careful fish dealer.

BAKED STUFFED WHITEFISH (or Arctic char)
2 tablespoons butter
2 medium onions, chopped
4 stalks celery, chopped, including leaves
2 teaspoons dillweed, dried OR 1 teaspoon chopped
  fresh dillweed
1 scant teaspoon salt
1/4 teaspoon black pepper
1-2 cups torn pieces of stale bread,
  white wine (optional)
  OR 2 tablespoons lemon juice
1 whole whitefish, about 6-7 pounds
1/2 cut lemon

Melt the butter in a saucepan, add the onion and celery and sauté till softened but still crunchy. Stir in the dill, salt and pepper and the bread and mix thoroughly. If the mixture seems a little dry, splash in some white wine. Remove from the heat and allow to cool. Wipe the fish inside and out with a clean damp cloth and rub the inside with a cut lemon. Lay the fish on a large pan, open the cavity and fill with as much of the stuffing as you can get into it. Thrust several skewers along the side of the opening and lace string among the skewers to hold the stuffing in.

Cover loosely with foil (but wrap the head tightly, if still on) and bake in a 375°F oven for 10 minutes per inch thickness of the fish, stuffing and all—about one hour. Remove the foil cover for the last 15 minutes. Serve whole on a platter garnished with lemon slices and parsley. A large piece of foil in the pan under the fish will make it easier to lift out, and the pan will be easier to clean. The same recipe works with an Arctic char.

I must admit, Amma, that these days when we are so weight-conscious, I often skip the stuffing and oven-poach a whole fish.

> *OVEN-POACHED FISH*
> (halibut, salmon, char, whitefish)
> *1 whole fish, about 6 or 7 pounds, scaled,*
> *   split and gutted*
> *salt and pepper*
> *1 whole lemon*
> *2 tablespoons dried dillweed*
> *a splash of dry white wine*

Lay the fish on a large piece of foil, big enough to wrap it in. Wipe it inside and out with a clean damp cloth. Sprinkle the insides of the fish with salt and black pepper to taste. Slice the lemon in thin slices and lay the slices in the cavity the length of the fish. Crush dried dillweed in your fingers and sprinkle it over the lemon slices. Bring the sides of the foil up ready to enclose the fish, but just before sealing it, pour the white wine over it. Seal the fish with a drugstore wrap (that is, triple folds so no liquid or steam can escape). Bake—or poach, really—at 375°F for 10 to 15 minutes per inch thickness, about one hour.

Then there's leftover fish. I guess Auntie Anna learned how to make *fiskabollur* (fish balls) from you, but it's her recipe I use. The only difference is, she used a meat grinder; I use a food processor.

> *FISKABOLLUR*
> *1 small onion, quartered*
> *2 cups (or so) leftover, cooked fish*
> *1/4 cup milk*
> *2 eggs, separated*
> *1 teaspoon salt (or less)*
> *1/4 teaspoon black pepper*
> *seasoned flour (with salt, pepper mixed into it)*
> *butter or margarine*

Drop the quartered onion into the bowl of a food processor and whirl it on and off to chop it. Add the fish, milk, egg yolks and salt and pepper seasoning and mix/chop together. In a separate bowl beat the egg whites to soft peaks and fold in the fish mixture. Now wet your hands or use a spoon to handle the glop. Take a heaping spoonful at a time and roll it in seasoned flour, shaping the stuff into 12 balls, flattening them slightly. Put them on wax paper on a cookie sheet and chill them for at least one hour. Sauté in butter or margarine until they are golden brown, turning as you see fit.

Serves 4 or 6, depending on how much your family likes fish balls. Good with beets or beet horseradish.

No one knows better than you, Amma, how much fish the Icelanders eat, and so do Western Icelanders unless they marry men like my father. When my cousins and I were moving around Iceland in the dark, everyone we visited fed us. For one thing they were all very hospitable; for another there were no restaurants outside of the major cities. I couldn't help noticing a certain similarity in a fish casserole we were served in almost every home. It's good, it is easily augmented if there are unexpected mouths to feed, and it is authentic, modern Icelandic cooking.

FISH CASSEROLE
1 large onion, diced
2 tablespoons butter or oil
1 teaspoon curry powder, or to taste
1 cup cooked rice
1 package of frozen fish, partially thawed OR
  fresh fish, cut into bite-sized chunks

Optional additions:
1 can pineapple chunks, with some of the juice
1 can corn niblets, drained
more rice
grated cheese for topping (not my preference with
  curry)
Major Grey Chutney on the side

Sauté the onion in the butter or oil until it has softened and stir in the curry powder to allow the heat to release the flavour. In a casserole combine the cooked rice, fish chunks and whatever else you want to add. Stir in the onion/curry mixture, moisten the mixture with pineapple juice or fish stock or white wine—something wet. Bake covered in a 350°F oven for 30 minutes or in a microwave oven, covered but vented for 6 or 7 minutes on High. Let stand covered for a minute or two when you take it out before serving. For some reason this dish tasted better in Iceland than it does in Canada; I think it must have been the fish.

While we're on the subject of fish, I'll give you cousin Hebba's recipe for *gravlax*. I have found old recipes using saltpetre, but it was used as a preservative and dates from the days when there was no refrigeration. Also, the small amount we're making here will be used up before there's any danger of it spoiling.

> *GRAVLAX*
> *1 teaspoon black peppercorns*
> *1 tablespoon sugar*
> *2 tablespoons (or less) salt*
> *1 bunch fresh dill OR $1/2$ to 1 cup dried dill*
> *1 pound salmon fillets in 2 pieces, skin on, deboned*
> *$1/2$ teaspoon lemon juice, if required*

Grind the peppercorns and mix with the sugar and salt. Lay out a large piece of foil considerably bigger than a salmon fillet. Lay down a thick bed of dill the same size as a fillet, then sprinkle it with the seasoning mixture. Place the first fillet skin side down on this prepared area, then do another number (dill and seasonings) on the upside of this fish. Lay the other fillet on top, skin side up, head-to-toe, that is, opposite, so as to make it come out an even thickness.

Sprinkle the rest of the seasonings on that and top with another thick layer of dill. If you feel like it, put lemon juice into the foil package before you seal it tightly with a drugstore wrap (triple folds so no juice can escape). I usually wait until the first time I open it and see how moist it is before adding the lemon juice.

Put the package in a pan with sides (in case it leaks), place a weight on it, not too heavy, and store it in the fridge. After 24 hours, turn the package over. If it has leaked, your package was not sealed tightly enough. Save the juice and pour it on the fish when you open the package.

After another 24 hours, turn it over again. This amount of fish will probably be ready to eat after 48 hours; it should be uniformly pickled and will look like a moist, smoked salmon. If it's not, or doesn't, give it another 12 hours. It will keep 7 to 10 days in the fridge, but someone will eat it all before the time is up. Keep it well sealed and add more lemon juice if it needs moistening. It will also keep up to 6 months in the freezer.

Serve with Icelandic Brown Bread or a good French bread and Mustard-Dill Sauce

MUSTARD-DILL SAUCE
1/4 cup Dijon mustard
1/4 cup honey mustard OR more Dijon, mixed with
1 teaspoon sugar
a few drops of olive oil
a bunch of fresh dill

Make this in a blender or a mini-food processor, if possible. If not, use the back of a spoon to mix the sugar and dill into the mustard with enough oil to bring it to an easy spreading consistency.

Another recipe that uses saltpetre is one of my favourite Icelandic preparations—*rúllupylsa*. Again, skipping a generation—my mother never made it. I used to make it every Christmas as a special holiday treat. The trick is to get good lamb breast. I keep the saltpetre in this recipe because that's what gives the meat its pink colour.

> *RÚLLUPYLSA*
> *2 1/4 pounds breast of lamb (probably two of them)*
> *1 tablespoon salt*
> *1 1/2 teaspoons saltpetre*
> *1/2 teaspoon ground cloves*
> *1/2 teaspoon ground allspice*
> *1/2 teaspoon black pepper*
> *2 tablespoons chopped onion*
> *water to cover*

Trim the meat, removing gristle and as much fat as possible, and lay it out flat. Mix the salt, saltpetre, cloves, allspice, pepper and onion together and spread the mixture over the meat. Starting on the long side, roll it up as if for a jelly roll. Tie the roll with pieces of string along the length of it to help it hold its shape. Put the roll into a deep saucepan with enough water to cover. Bring the water to a boil, skim off any froth or fat, simmer for 15 minutes. Pull the roll out of the water and put it between two smooth surfaces (a couple of plates?), with a heavy weight on top (a couple of books?). Allow to season in a cold place for a day. The cold place need not be the fridge; it can be a cold closet, an unheated sunroom, even the garage—but beware of foraging animals!

To serve, remove the strings and cut into thin slices. Good with Icelandic Brown Bread.

Although I like liver, I was never very fond of *lifrapylsa*. The original recipe calls for stuffing the meat mixture into some kind of container, at one time the stomach and duodenum of a sheep. The meat was, of course, sheep liver. I've heard it said of Mennonites that they use every part of a goose but the honk; I think Icelanders used every part of the sheep but the bleat. Later, people used tubelike casings made from white cotton, soaked in cold water and then stuffed with the meat filling. Nowadays, I guess stockinet would serve, but I chose an easier method. I pack it into a meat loaf pan and bake it. I thought this was original but my cousin Lorna says that's what she does and she offered an improvement in the cooking process.

> *LIFRAPYLSA*
> *2 pounds beef liver*
> *3/4 pound suet*
> *1 cup milk*
> *1/2 teaspoon black pepper*
> *1 1/2 tablespoons salt*
> *1/4 teaspoon allspice*
> *1/4 teaspoon ground cloves*
> *1 cup oatmeal*
> *1 cup whole wheat flour*

Put the liver and suet into the bowl of a food processor (failing that, use a meat grinder or a blender in several go rounds) and whirl until it is a consistent, disgusting-looking mess. Scald the milk and add it to the mixture in the bowl along with the pepper, salt, allspice, cloves and the oatmeal and flour and blend it all together. It should have a consistency of a thick cake batter or a wet meat loaf mixture. This mixture can be stuffed into wet cotton casings, tied shut and dropped into boiling, salted water for two hours. Take out the bags and slit them down the side while they're still hot; the meat will come out in one piece, ready for slicing.

Using my easy method, pack the meat mixture into a

greased loaf pan and bake at 350°F for one hour. Lorna sets the pan into a larger, shallow one and pours boiling water into that. Then she bakes the loaf for about 2 hours in a 350°F oven. This method results in a moister loaf.

Serve hot, like a meat loaf, with baked potatoes and plenty of ketchup or salsa. Some cooks fry leftover slices in butter but I think that's overdoing it. I like it better in sandwiches, sliced very thin, with a good hot mustard.

There's no doubt that Icelanders have a sweet tooth, and our family is no exception. How could we help it, with a baker like you in the family, Amma? Afi's second store—the Breeze Inn at the north end of the main street—was called the north store by the family because it was north of the big store, and it added to your workload and loyal fans by offering your fabulous pies for sale. The small store was more like a soda shop. There were a few tables in the back which I remember only because on rainy days a friend and I would sit at one of them playing with the Eaton's catalogue, making paper dolls and dressing them from the clothing pages, and furnishing rooms by pasting pictures of furniture on a big sheet of paper. You gave us scissors and made flour-and-water paste for us, and then a piece of your home-made pie each for our hard work. Your pies must have been big sellers: lemon meringue, raisin, apple. How did you do it?

Pie does not come to mind, though, as an Icelandic speciality, nor was it your most popular item with the family. *Vínar terta*, the surprising "Vienna torte," is still the single best-known and best-loved food that everyone associates with Icelandic cooking, but I discovered to my surprise that it's no big deal in Iceland. Only in North America has the love of *vínar terta* and the arguments about its authentic taste made it the single most important item on any Thorrablót menu. Outsiders are taken aback by the filling—prunes instead of Viennese *schlag*—but soon pass on the whipped cream. There are several schools of thought about the filling and the flavouring. Lazy cooks spread jam between the cookie-like layers; some put almond flavouring in the filling instead of in the cake dough; others put cinnamon instead of cardamom in the prune filling.

In its web site section on Icelandic recipes the Icelandic National League identifies *vínar terta* as a "special occasion cake." Certainly it was for me when I learned to make it. It usually took me about two days to assemble it and then it must ripen for at least a day for the best taste. I used to make it at Christmastime instead of a fruit cake. But you, Amma, you must have made one at least once a week. I can't remember a coffee break without it.

You were gone by the time I took an interest in Icelandic cooking. It wasn't until I was married, and even then, not until I was gathering material for my *Gourmet* article about your cooking, that I finally made *vínar terta*. I scavenged recipes from an old Dorcas Society cookbook—a booklet, really—privately published as a fundraiser, and from Auntie Anna. I guess you taught her how.

> AUNTIE ANNA'S VÍNAR TERTA
> ¾ cup butter
> 2 cups sugar
> 3 eggs, beaten
> Mix together:
>   ½ teaspoon almond flavouring
>   1 tablespoon water
>   4 tablespoons evaporated milk
> 5 cups flour
> 2 teaspoons baking powder
> 1 teaspoon salt

Cream the butter and sugar together, then blend in the eggs and flavouring. Sift the flour with the baking powder and salt and add alternately with the water/milk mixture, blending well after each addition, totalling three. The ultimate texture will be that of a cookie dough, as opposed to a cake dough. On a floured board, roll and cut 8-inch or 10-inch circles of dough, depending on the size of the cake pans they are to be baked in. Bake 5 to 8 minutes in a 400°F oven. These layers should be quite thin. There should be 12 cake-size cookies ready to assemble into two six-layer cakes.

> PRUNE FILLING
> 2 pounds medium-size dried prunes, cooked and
>   pitted (according to the package directions)
> 1 teaspoon ground cardamom
> 2 1/2 cups sugar

Put the pitted, cooked prunes through a meat grinder (olden days) or drop them in the food processor with the cardamom and sugar and blend to a smooth, spreading consistency. Build two cakes, each layer spread with the filling except the last, top, one. If desired, the cakes can be frosted with a plain vanilla icing. Let the cakes ripen—until the cookie layers soften—for at least a day before serving. The extra cake will keep well in the freezer. (A word to the uninitiated about cutting this cake. Do not cut it into standard wedges like an ordinary layer cake. Instead, cut it into inch-and-a-half-wide pieces about 1 inch thick—like a fruit cake. It's very rich. You can always have a second piece.)

The other classic Icelandic food known to the outside world is *Pönnukökur*—Icelandic pancakes—not crêpes, not blini, but just as thin and just as delicious in their way, served with their traditional fillings.

PÖNNUKÖKUR
1/2 teaspoon baking soda
1/2 cup sour cream
1/2 teaspoon salt
1/2 teaspoon nutmeg OR 1/2 teaspoon cinnamon
    (my choice) OR 1/2 teaspoon almond extract and
1 teaspoon vanilla, added to the milk
1 teaspoon baking powder
1/4 cup white sugar
2 cups flour
2 eggs
2 cups milk

Stir the baking soda into the sour cream to let it bubble. Add the salt and spice of choice along with the baking powder and sugar to the flour. Beat the eggs, stir in the sour-cream mixture and blend this mixture into the dry mixture. Add the almond and vanilla flavouring (if using) to the milk and stir until everything is moistened and blended, but do not overbeat. Bake as preferred on a hot fry pan or seasoned griddle, using fat as desired (I don't). Stack the pancakes between layers of paper towels and keep them warm until all the batter is used. Then sprinkle each pancake with brown sugar (some people use icing sugar) and roll up. You'll notice I give you a choice of seasoning; people can come to blows over their preference. I don't want to hear about it.

I prefer brown sugar, because that's the way you served them, Amma. Others like a mixture of white sugar and cinnamon. For festive occasions, like a Thorrablót, the pancakes are spread with thickly whipped cream and a dollop of jam, then folded into quarters, but these have to be eaten with a fork. Of course, in my frugal Western Icelandic fashion, I use up my leftover buttermilk pancakes in this way, rolling them up with brown sugar and pretending it was on purpose.

Icelandic doughnuts are really dough *knots*, and more fun than plasticine to shape. They are another staple of coffee time. I season mine with nutmeg, rather than the more familiar cinnamon. Do you know, Amma, I still have your nutmeg grater? I always buy whole nutmegs and grate them as needed; the difference in flavour is remarkable, so I remark it.

> *KLEINUR*
> *1 cup sour cream*
> *1 cup milk*
> *2 teaspoons baking soda*
> *1 teaspoon salt*
> *1 teaspoon nutmeg*
> *1 teaspoon cream of tartar*
> *4 cups (approx.) flour*
> *3 eggs*
> *1 1/2 cups sugar*
> *1 teaspoon vanilla*
> *deep fat for frying, that is, about 3 inches of oil or*
> *   lard in a deep skillet*

Mix the sour cream with the milk and stir in the baking soda to give it time to work. Add the salt, nutmeg and cream of tartar to 3 cups of the flour and sift them together. Now beat the eggs, adding sugar slowly to them to make it a smooth mixture, and stirring in the vanilla. Then add the sour-cream mixture and the flour mixture in alternative additions, about one cup of each at a time, blending well. When the dough is fairly stiff, drop it onto a board with the remaining cup of flour and knead it lightly, adding more flour if necessary. Divide the dough into three parts and work with one at a time. Roll it out to about ¼-inch thickness, cut into inch-wide strips and these into 2 ½-inch-long pieces. Pick up a piece and put a slit in the centre, then pull one end through the slit. A knot! Proceed with the rest of the dough.

In the meantime, heat the fat or oil (I prefer peanut oil as it's slightly less flammable; some people use lard; others Crisco) to about 375°F on a thermometer. Drop as many knots as will comfortably fit in the fryer and turn them as needed, frying until they are golden brown. Lift and drain the knots on brown paper laid on cookie sheets or an impervious counter, and keep frying. Sieve icing sugar over them before serving. Makes about two dozen, depending on the size.

Ástarbollur were invented before TimBits®. It's the same idea—deep-fat frying—but a different shape, with a few raisins thrown in for fun.

> ÁSTARBOLLUR
> 2 tablespoons soft butter
> 3/4 cup sugar
> 2 eggs beaten
> 2/3 cup milk
> 1 teaspoon vanilla
> 2 cups flour
> 1/2 teaspoon salt
> 2 teaspoons baking power
> 1/2 teaspoon nutmeg
> 1/2 cup raisins
> oil or fat for frying, about three inches in a deep
>   skillet
> 1/2 cup sugar
> 1/2 teaspoon cinnamon

Cream the butter and sugar and stir in the beaten eggs. Add the milk and vanilla. Sift the flour, salt, baking powder and nutmeg together into a bowl and stir the raisins into it to coat them so they won't clump in one place in the batter. Stir this mixture into the first one. Drop the batter into hot (375°F) fat or oil with a teaspoon.

Dip the teaspoon into the hot oil each time before taking up the next scoop of batter, it will slide off more easily. Don't try to fry too many at a time, only as many as are comfortable in the fryer. Give them room to bounce around and turn by themselves. If they don't turn, nudge them. Drain on several layers of brown paper, and while still hot, roll them in a mixture of sugar and cinnamon.

I have a fear of frying for several reasons: an aversion to cholesterol, a cautionary attitude towards fat fires, and a dislike of a house that smells like a greasy spoon. The odour does linger. Also, it's very hot work, hanging over deep fat. When I think of you, Amma, cooking over a wood-burning stove in the heat of summer, my heart melts. I also remember you used to move down to your "summer kitchen," the cool, stone-walled basement where the warm-hearted little laundry stove supplied your cooking needs. It had to be 20° cooler down there. Remembering that, I used to serve dinner in the basement of our first house when it got too hot in Winnipeg in the summer.

I didn't realize when I was first married how hot cooking can be, until I did my first deep-fat frying. Ensconced in our first little apartment, I was slowly equipping the kitchen for what I thought I would need to be a good cook. One day on a shopping expedition I found some rosette irons. I could not resist—rosette irons. They look like small branding irons, but in very un-ranchlike shapes, usually butterfly or flower cut-outs, on the end of a long handle. The idea is to heat the branding iron in hot fat, dip it quickly into batter, plunge it again into the fat and fry the shape until it lets go, floats in the fat and fries until it's done—golden brown. Then lift the rosette out and drain it on brown paper, letting it cool while you dip and fry some more. The results are those lovely vehicles for jam and whipped cream I remember you giving me for a special treat in the afternoon.

> *ROSETTES*
> *2 eggs*
> *1 teaspoon white sugar*
> *1/4 teaspoon salt*
> *1 cup milk*
> *1 cup flour*
> *deep fat for frying (lard, shortening or peanut oil)*

Beat the eggs lightly with the sugar and salt. Add the milk and flour, beat until smooth. Follow my description, being careful not to let the batter ride over the top of the iron. It doesn't take long to fry the rosettes, the batter is so thin—maybe 20-30 seconds. If it doesn't slide off the iron, okay; use paper towelling or an old tea towel (to prevent burnt fingers) to slip the rosette off the iron. Some purists sprinkle icing sugar on their rosettes, no jam or whipped cream. That's good too.

But oh, the heat! And the work! I didn't make rosettes again for about 14 years. The thing is, you have to love what you're doing. If I'm going to do it at all, I'm going to save my energy and fat for *laufabrauð*.

Do you know, Amma, I had never heard of *laufabrauð* before I went to Iceland at Christmastime? Then it's impossible to avoid it. Every household I went into served it, and at Brekka, where I stayed to visit the Glaumbær Museum, I was allowed to help. After that, when I went into Akureyri, I bought a *laufabrauð* cutter at a bakery. A *laufabrauð* cutter is like a pie or pizza-cutter, a little cutting wheel on a handle, but this wheel is brass and three-dimensional, shaped like a barrel with a deep-relief design on it in a chevron pattern. When it's rolled over a circle of dough it cuts impressions in it which, when the dough is fried, puff up into various designs, depending on which way it is cut. A finished *laufabrauð* looks like a fried doily. Some people, instead of eating them, hang "doilies" in their windows as a Christmas decoration. They're fun to make and fun to eat. I've made a batch with my grandchildren since that trip. I have to keep doing it because the *laufabrauð* cutter cost so much! Maybe that's why you didn't own one, Amma; it's not the most necessary item to take with one across the ocean at the age of 17.

> *LAUFABRAUÐ*
> *4 cups flour*
> *2 tablespoons sugar*
> *1 tablespoon salt*
> *1 teaspoon baking powder*
> *3 cups milk*
> *1/4 cup butter*
> *oil (or lard) for frying*

Combine the flour, sugar, salt and baking powder in a large bowl. Heat the milk and butter together until the butter melts. Blend into the dry ingredients and stir well. Flour a board or countertop generously, dump the dough on it and roll out very, very thin. Cut the dough into rounds about the size of a salad plate (8 inches in diameter). Hand out circles to people to take their turns at decorating. Roll the cutter over the dough (some people use a knife or scissors if they're impatient) and create interesting effects. Deep-fry in hot oil (my Icelandic relatives used lard) until golden brown on both sides, turning once, or not, depending on how it looks.

It's a lovely family activity and there's no such thing as a failure. They all get eaten—or hung up.

There were two foods that you served regularly, Amma, that I had to acquire a taste for in my adult years: *skyr* and *mysostur*. *Skyr* is Iceland's answer to yogurt and it's kind of like yogurt or maybe German quark, a relatively low-fat dairy product, depending on the milk used. It was the chief staple in the diet of the earliest inhabitants, more often made with sheep's or goat's milk in the early days, and eaten with porridge, maybe occasionally a little fish, and something to ward off scurvy (lichen or seaweed?). *Skyr* varies; it can be very sour, creamy or not so, most commonly about the same texture as sour cream. It's served at breakfast with or without fruit and/or cereal, cold or cooked. It's dessert at other meals, by itself or with fruit. Here's a recipe for *skyr*. I chose the easiest one I could find, made from buttermilk.

SKYR[3]

Pour two cartons of buttermilk into a wide bowl and set it in an oven that has been warmed (to about 200°F) and then turned off. Leave the buttermilk in the oven with the light on for about 12 hours, after which the whey should be visibly separating from the curd. Line a colander with an old tea towel (I use a new J-cloth® and set it over a stockpot or some other big pail-like container.) Pour the buttermilk very gently over the cloth and let it drain like that for about 4 hours, or until the curd is fairly firm. The curd is what remains in the cloth. Put the curd in a bowl and beat it until it's

---

3 This recipe is taken from the Icelandic Canadian newspaper, *Logberg-Heimskringla*, submitted by Ron Eyolfson.

smooth. Add sugar to taste. Some people like it served with cream.

One of those electric yogurt makers that were all the rage a few years ago could also be used. They can be found in garage sales. I have to tell you, Amma, no one I met in Iceland made her own *skyr*. Cousin Hebba, like everyone else, buys it, either from the supermarket or from her favourite dairy store. In the New World there isn't enough demand for it, so people have to make their own.

The word *mysostur* comes from *mysa*, whey, and it's a kind of easy, cooked spread considered to be cheese, because *ostur* means cheese. I avoided it when you served it, but I love it now. It's better in Iceland than here and so common it's included in the little basket of those individual-serving tubs of jam, honey, peanut butter and marmalade. Failing the authentic Icelandic version, here is a simple method for making it at home.

> *MYSOSTUR*
> *2 cups dark brown sugar*
> *2 cups whey powder*
> *1 can (385mL) evaporated milk*
> *1 tablespoon butter*

Combine the sugar, whey powder and milk in the top part of a double boiler and stir well to break down any lumps in the sugar, and blend in the whey. Cook over gently boiling water for 2 or 3 hours, stirring occasionally, being sure the mixture doesn't get lumpy or grainy as it thickens. When it is good and thick, remove from the heat and allow to cool slightly. Then stir in the butter, allow it to melt and stir again to prevent graininess. Put in a jar and refrigerate. It can be frozen, but that isn't really necessary. Serve as a spread on whole wheat crackers or toast. It's also good with celery sticks or with fresh Bosc pears.

In his fascinating book, *The Icelandic Heritage*,[4] historian Nelson S. Gerrard describes the food early Icelanders ate. With the limited resources of the country, the people lived on a subsistence-level diet for centuries. Breakfast and the evening meal was usually *skyr*, with fresh milk in the summer and hot gruel in the winter, made from ryemeal, or *grasagrautur*— grass gruel made from lichen. I guess that prevented scurvy. In season, there might be a few berries: blueberries or the indigenous kraekiberries, to add a little taste.

I found a recipe for grass custard in an Icelandic Canadian cooking brochure, but I'm sure it was offered as an historical curiosity. The cook, Margret Geppért, calls the lichen *fjallagr*ös, or mountain grasses, apparently using the terms lichen and grass interchangeably. In the cook-booklet printed by the Leif Eiriksson Icelandic Club of Calgary,[5] she tells us that in the old days in Iceland an entire family would pick the grasses on damp spring nights. Then they made the gruel Gerrard referred to or added it to *bló∂m*ör, for which I refuse to give a recipe (a kind of blood sausage). Here's Margret Geppért's recipe for

> *FJALLAGRASAMJÓLK* (Lichen Custard)
> *40 grams lichen*
> *1 1/2 quarts of milk*
> *1 teaspoon salt*
> *1 tablespoon brown sugar*

Wash the grasses in cold water and clean away any pieces of moss. I'm not making this up; I'm quoting Margret

---

4 *op. cit.*
5 "Recipes," edited by Freda Abrahamson, 1988.

Geppért. Boil the milk and stir in the grasses. Cook for 5 minutes. Add salt and sugar—I was going to say "to taste," but why? Margret Geppért adds a comment: "If this is boiled a bit longer, the milk thickens. Serve as a dessert or with sour blood pudding or with red currant pudding."

In her book of poetry[6] inspired by the early settlers, Canadian poet and novelist Kristjana Gunnars, who was born in Iceland and is a first-generation settler, describes this gruel/porridge/custard in one of her poems:

> *...iceland moss porridge*
> *keeps you alive even*
> *if you don't like to look*

Nelson Gerrard concludes his description of the meagre diet of the Icelanders with an acknowledgement of *fjallagrös*. He says that mountain grass was often what stood between the people and total starvation. He says many people subsisted on this in times of famine, plus dried seaweed—*söl*, what we call dulse. At least they never had a goitre.

For the midday meal, Nelson Gerrard continues, there might be a little meat, more often fish than animal, fresh fish if there was a nearby stream, which there usually was. I don't even want to talk about *hákarl* (shark), which had to be aged, to put it mildly, in order for it to be edible and safe to consume. Gerrard says it had to be cut up and hung for a year; our bus driver, who was sadistically offering pieces of it to his passenger , said it should be buried until it smells like urine. The piece I got passed that test. Much more palatable was *harðfiskur*, hardfish or air-dried fish chewed with butter.

Butter was important. Did you know, Amma, that at one time it was a unit of currency in the economy? Salted

6 *Settlement Poems I*, Winnipeg: Turnstone Press, 1980.

butter, though fresher-tasting, didn't keep as well, surprisingly; unsalted butter could go sour without harming anyone and could be kept as long as 20 years. Icelandic butter was usually a combination of both cow's and sheep's milk, with the preference going to the sheep's product. It was usually spread on some kind of bread, usually *flatbrauð*—essentially flour, oatmeal, some kind of leaven and water, that was mixed, flattened and baked on a griddle until brown on both sides, or, simpler than that, Poor Man's Bread: flour, milk and baking powder, mixed and baked in a bread pan in a hot oven till brown.

If there was meat, it was usually mutton. Hung meat *(hangikjöt*—originally meat hung from the kitchen rafters to smoke from the fire below) was considered a treat then and now. Now you can buy it packaged in deli slices in the grocery store, but finer stores sell whole hocks for a festive meal, usually served with those caramelized potatoes Auden hated.

Those early inhabitants of Iceland, sitting in their *baðstofa*, the communal room, telling stories, eating their *skyr*, had few possessions. One item each person owned was his or her bowl and spoon. The bowl was made of wood for the very young and the very old so they shouldn't break their dish, originally ash wood, whence it derived its name: *askur*. It usually had a wooden, hinged lid that helped to keep the food warm and it was intricately carved on the outside, frequently with the person's name or some distinctive design. The spoon was usually made of bone or pewter, nothing breakable. Of course, these were precious possessions because without them, one could not eat.

Today *askurs* are highly regarded, and commemorative ones are often awarded to someone who has served the community. They continue to be made by skilled craftspeople and are sold in craft stores, where they are kept under lock and key and brought out for inspection only upon request. I made such a request and brought home an *askur* from my Christmas trip to Iceland. I noticed, when I first discovered *askurs* in people's living rooms in Iceland, that their owners are inclined to use them as informal catchalls for paper clips, ticket stubs, bits of ribbon and other unclassifiable clutter. I keep mine empty, ready for food—not grass gruel, though.

That was there and then, this is here and now. Think of what you found here, Amma: all kinds of berries, like saskatoons and huckleberries, wild raspberries, strawberries and red currants. Blueberries, both wild and domestic, are everywhere, good for pies and muffins and to stir into *pönnukökur*. Corn, on and off the cob, was new to you, and peas in the pod, I think. I remember shelling them for you and you would run them quickly by the stove so that they were scarcely cooked, hot and very tender. Leaf lettuce I have already mentioned, and all the sweet root vegetables that came out of the good Manitoba earth. And then there were all those fish!

The first fish caught in Nyja Ísland, according to one historian, was a goldeye. The fisherman's wife cooked it and found it to be soggy and bland. I wonder who the genius was who thought of smoking it. That thought put smoked goldeye on the gourmet map of the world. We have to be careful, though. Buyers are told always to buy smoked goldeye with the head on so as to be reassured by the sight of that golden eye. Otherwise, they'll be sold tullibee, which is a poor relation. Besides the big Lake Winnipeg whitefish, there were sunfish, now endangered, as were the goldeye and pickerel, a fish much smaller than Lake Superior pike. For a time Lake Winnipeg's fish, along with other fish in freshwater lakes of the world, were threatened with mercury poisoning, toxins from fertilizers, all sorts of chemical stews. Tougher laws and embargoes are slowly bringing them back to edible levels.

To my knowledge we had no fishermen in the family, neither commercial nor sporting, except my mother, who liked to sit with a fishing rod. I never knew her to catch a fish. Your sons, my uncles Pete and Joe and Bob, were hunters. Bob had a dog who loved hunting and who took his master out every fall. Terry tells me his father Joe was considered the best duck hunter in Gimli and environs, but no one ever told me that Uncle Pete shot the moose whose head still hangs in Tergesen's store. I have known other hunters though my husband was not one, I'm happy to say. Still, I've had enough wild ducks given to me that I've learned how to cook them. Put Manitoba mallard on the gourmet map, too, especially with this simple recipe:

BREAST OF MALLARD
breasts and tenderloins of mallard ducks,
   at least one duck per person
a favourite stuffing recipe
red wine OR chicken stock

If the hunter has been eagle-eyed, the cook can afford to take all the ducks bagged and not bother plucking or cleaning them. Just cut out the breasts and tenderloins, wipe well and lay aside while preparing the stuffing. Put a layer of stuffing in the bottom of a fairly deep, greased casserole and then put in a layer of meat. More stuffing, more meat, carrying on until all the meat is used up, and finishing off with a top layer of stuffing. Pour red wine or chicken stock over the contents to moisten everything. Cover and bake 1 1/2 hours in a 350°F oven. Serve with wild rice, another Manitoba gourmet treat.

There are lovely birds in Iceland, several species I had never seen before, including the puffin or *lundi*. People near the coast hunted the birds' eggs, and used the down for coverlets. The puffin was and is still a special culinary treat. Just days after I had seen my first puffin in the wilds, I was back in Reykjavik when my cousin Halldóra invited me for dinner at Perlan, the elegant revolving restaurant above the gigantic hot-water storage cylinders on the east side of Reykjavik. She took Hebba and Hreggviður, too, not only because they were family but also because we needed interpreters. Hebba ordered puffin. They were medallions, beautifully cooked, I expect, but I couldn't watch her eat them.

I've already told the story of Drángey Island with its rich supply of birds and eggs. The ptarmigan *(rjúpa)* is also popular, the bird of choice for the traditional Christmas dinner. It's a land bird, more like our grouse. There seem to have been no domesticated fowl. What would those poor birds have eaten?

It's a sad but familiar story, the way the language and culture of the old country fade in the New World. While the first generation had to learn English as a second language, later generations have to make an effort to learn the "first" language—in special courses or interest groups. The culture often suffers the same fate. Western Icelanders are fortunate because their past is so rich; the sagas remain a respectable literature that cultivated people should know. The easiest way for most of us to hang onto the past, however, is through the food. I guess that's why Thorrablót is so popular throughout North America, wherever there is an Icelandic or a Scandinavian club. And I guess that's why arguments can become so heated about the right way to make *vínar terta*. And it's also why I become so nostalgic, Amma, as I recall the introduction you gave me to Icelandic food. I hope others enjoy our culinary trip down memory lane.

—YOUR LOVING GRANDDAUGHTER, BETTY JANE

CANTO TWO
—LETTER TO W.H. AUDEN

I guess that some delights at first may look
Bizarre. With words like gross and horrible
You made it very clear throughout your book
You thought Icelandic food deplorable.
Remember food was never storable
In olden times, so it was smoked or soured.
When folks were hungry it was all devoured.

I learned to hanker after hangikjöt—
That's lamb left hanging in a smoky rafter—
Though buried shark meat leaves me quite inert
Because it smells like pee the morning after.
I think, although the food is cause for laughter,
A taste acquired from necessity
Will soon be savoured with alacrity.

The sagas, too, bear some consideration,
Those violent tales of families in strife
From harsher times when the least aberration
Could cost a man his chattels and his life
And one reward of battle was his wife.
I question the unfairness to the bride.
I always want to take the woman's side.

(I read there's fewer women now than men,
A fact I cannot easily forgive.

It comes as no surprise to learn that when
People can choose which sex they want to live
They opt for male. The reason that they give
Is females live so long in any case
Men need a handicap to win the race.)

Another thing—the rocks and ice, I mean.
A large part of the charm of northern climes
Is rugged land with nothing in between
(No grass to cut.) I find that water primes
The pump of art, that is to say—sometimes.
You had no need of outside inspiration
For which you have my heartfelt admiration.

You spent three months in touring on a horse
Long before the Ring Road was begun.
I toured the first time in a bus, of course;
I took three weeks, and thought it quite a bargain.
It would have helped if I had known the jargon.
But still I found that Iceland left its mark
So I went back to see it in the dark.

Forgive me, then, for adding my own spin
To your fine travelogue and observations.
The joy of any trip comes from within.
Discovering one has no reservations—
And I don't mean hotel—the celebrations
Of self arise from scrutiny of place.
The fun's not in arrival but the chase.

—BJW

CHAPTER SEVEN

COMFORT
—LETTER TO MY COUSIN'S COUSIN

DEAR HELGA:

You are my cousin's cousin on his mother's side so I guess that makes us close—not blood, but kin—and gives me the right to address a letter to you. In any case, you'll be interested in my encounter with an Icelandic museum because the office where you preside as secretary of the Icelandic National League is over the Heritage Museum in Gimli. One good tour deserves another.

It was the shortest day of the year, December 22, the winter solstice, when I visited the museum at Glaumbær which is a sod "manor house," so-called because of its size. It's open only in the summer months—what fool would want to shiver through it in the winter? Our resource-ful cousin Lorna had arranged for her and Terry and me to meet a young woman named Sigríður Sigurðardóttir, the curator of Glaumbær Museum, and also of the Immigration Museum at Hofsos. Glaumbaer is a 20-minute drive from Brekka, the farm where Lorna had also thoughtfully arranged for us to stay (with kin), so as to be able to make this visit.

Normally I'm very good at guessing time, accurate with-in five or ten minutes, but that December I had totally lost my sense of it. It looked and felt like midnight but it was only about 5:30 p.m. when we rattled into the farmyard of Glaumbær on the protesting wheels of a car that would have preferred its warm garage to a frozen road. My choice of time and date may have been deliberate, but I had not planned on the cold: -16°C, much colder than normal, I was told, even for northern Iceland.

Lights shone from the main farmhouse, used partly for display (the upstairs loft rooms); partly as office, housing the computer and files of the curator; salesroom, a counter offering postcards depicting Glaumbær; and restaurant, a delightful home kitchen for which I would soon be grateful when we returned for hot chocolate and *kleinur* (doughnuts). Across the yard darkness cloaked the manor, one of the largest turf houses ever built in Iceland—in the mid-19th century and actually occupied until 1946. If this sounds surprisingly recent, you have to remember that turf doesn't last as long as stone; the building was not that old.[1] Sigriður armed herself with a big flashlight and brandished a key, preparing to lead us into the past.

Modelled after the old sod houses the early inhabitants built with very little wood and a lot of turf, the dwelling at Glaumbær is a mansion with 16 rooms and a painted wooden facade on the front boasting windows and six entrances. Five of these open on single spaces: storerooms, fuel storage, a smithy, a guest room. The main entrance has a small second floor with another window—some kind of loft. The front of the house looks like an ordinary one-storey, clapboard building with a couple of dormer windows. Except for the front, the entire house is made of sod; from the side it looks like a long earth mound. An earth-floored, windowless corridor is carpeted in some kind of felt probably for the sake of tourists, whether to keep them from wearing down the "floor" or to keep their feet clean, I don't know. This hallway leads from the entrance through to the back of the house to the *baðstofa*— sleeping quarters cum family room—with separate rooms

---

1 There is, in a valley to the east of Reykjavik, a restored sod dwelling dating from the 12th century.

opening off each side on the way, thickly spaced with their earth walls; you can't cantilever sod. These rooms include the dairy, the pantry, the cooking room—the only room with fire in it—where the food was cooked, but not prepared, and, next to the communal hall, a room with a door to the outside, providing a fire escape route and usually housing farm animals in the winter. The animals supplied body heat. I would have welcomed them. Apparently no one complained of the smell. Lacking both smell and warmth, I was cold. By the time I stumbled from the dark turf house onto the frozen clods of the snow-covered track, cold cramps wracked my body. The light from the farmhouse spilled across the yard, promising 20th-century warmth, but my eyes were still focused on another era. The dark corridor behind me seemed like a time-travel entry point to another place. I had known it would be.

I had moved with race memory through that hallway, with its service rooms on either side, to the long T-bar of the *baðstofa*, the room where everything happened, across the back of the dwelling. Sigriður's flashlight had barely made a pocket in the black shroud of Glaumbær, yet I could see by the light of my mind's eye the people sitting on their beds and hear them talking, my shivers attuned to theirs. Actually, they were probably warmer than I was. With very few windows, the sod walls kept out the wind and concentrated the animal heat from the livestock. The only fire was in the central cooking room but there was also heat from others' bodies. From 22 to 30 people could sleep in the *baðstofa*.[2] Two more bedrooms, one at each end, with double, curtained bunks and windows, offered private but colder accommodation. Sigriður said the parents used to send the children to bed early to warm up the mattresses. Eleven lower bunks on each side line the walls at

---

2 The guidebooks report that because the air in Iceland is relatively bacteria-free, body odours were not particularly offensive. Who can argue? I bet they didn't perspire much, either.

Glaumbær, with a partial wooden wall separating each one, and each equipped with a decorated board called a *rúmfjöl,* usually carved with a prayer or blessing which was invoked as it was pushed down to tuck the covers tightly between the mattress and the outside frame. This board, across the knees, also served as dining and work table, and it provided fallout protection, like the barrier in an upper berth designed to keep the sleeping occupant from tumbling onto the floor. People slept two to a bed, head and feet alternating, men and boys on one side of the room, women and girls on the other, the window side, if there were windows.

Windows were a wasteful extravagance; not only was glass scarce and expensive, but too good a conductor of cold. Earlier windows were made of tough, unbreakable cows' bladders[3] stretched translucently thin to provide some light and conducting less cold, apparently. In winter or in night-time darkness, of course, light had to be created, supplied for centuries not by expensive, clear beeswax or even cheaper, smoky, tallow candles but by some sort of oil or fat. Women were given the best light, since their work demanded it: spinning, weaving, sewing and knitting, the latter task for everyone, male, female, young and old. The men had nets to mend (if they were fishermen) or ropes to make, and wool to comb, requiring less close work and therefore less light. And then there was a designated reader, the narrator whose role and function dated back centuries when a storyteller entertained people while they worked, kept the dark at bay and lit the flame within each spirit. Reading time was called *koldvaka*—cold wake, literally—the activity required to keep one awake in the chilly shadows while the work went on.

You're probably wondering, Helga, what happened to privacy or property? Granted, people owned little of value

---

3 A cow's bladder in Icelandic is a *skjar*. Remember that word!

or in their own right, but what little they had must have been precious. Such crowded and confined quarters (for such long periods) had to generate a strict code of behaviour. A covenant of privacy existed among the occupants of the sleeping hall. Although there were some shelves, personal belongings were usually kept under the pillow and were supposed to be as safe from snooping or theft as if they had been in a strongbox. Even so, people slept on their possessions, thus often forced, if they owned a lot, to sleep pretty high, propped up as they were by their things—sometimes almost upright. When this happened, they were described as "having a lot under them."

The *baðstofa* of a big farm would accommodate most of the people working on it, bound there by law (from the 15th century). If a widow or a child was left alone with no family, social assistance came from within the community. Homeless people were accommodated at a farm to live and work. People were seldom alone in their living arrangements. Many of the later tales involve the person left behind to mind the fire when everyone went to attend church, for example, on Christmas Eve. Only an innocent girl with her wits about her could withstand the attempts of elves or trolls to invade the place and drive her mad. The number of tales about this situation tells us how seldom that hall was empty of people.

I dwell on all these arrangements, the lack of light and privacy, because they led me to further speculations and conclusions about comfort and creation. I had to see for myself in order to validate my hunches. Only mad dogs and Englishmen go out in the noonday sun, according to Noel Coward's song, while the natives prefer a siesta. Icelanders, not even the ancient ones, are not known for siestas, nor, I think, for early bedtimes. They had too much night work to do. So they are all awake and listening while someone tells a story. Suspended in time, caught in that flickering light, mesmerized by the moving images created by the storyteller, they are not sleeping. I know that over the centuries many of them were hungry; I do think, however, that they were warm enough.

In his book, *Home,* Canadian architect and author Witold Rybczynski examines the idea of comfort, which is a relatively new concept in the history of human survival and which differs over centuries and civilizations depending on what facilities are available. As Rybczynski points out, all the modern inventions which have contributed to high domestic comfort and ease, such as central heating, indoor plumbing, running hot and cold water, electric light and power (tools, elevators, stairs) scarcely existed before 1890 and were astonishingly familiar by 1920. Now we live as aliens not only to a huge proportion of people in the world today, but also to those in the near and distant past. I am intensely interested to know how these changes have affected not only the psyche but the creative impulse.

What constitutes comfort? Where did the idea come from? Architecture is, after all, about providing shelter and one assumes, therefore, comfort to the creatures living within walls rather than under trees or in caves. Examining the idea of comfort, however, Rybczynski reports that when he was studying architecture, the concept came up only once, in relation to temperature: room thermometers are often marked with a "comfort zone"—somewhere between 68 and 72°F. Those of us who live in an intemperate climate know how important warmth is to a creature's comfort. Oddly enough—not oddly, but surprisingly to those who know little about the country—Iceland is one of the most comfortable countries in the world to live in, that is, I want to say, if one lives indoors. Thanks to all the geothermal energy lurking beneath the surface, Icelanders enjoy warmth, light, power and hot water in abundance, all the creature comforts at relatively little cost to the inhabitants, so little that they can afford to be lavish. Their energy consumption is reported to be the third highest in the world. That's today. But if Snorri Sturluson had a private hot tub at Reykholt in the 13th century, I bet some of those people in their sod huts had access to a few hot pools of their own.

I read a collection of outlaw stories[4] and I noticed that the Icelandic marauders in the tales didn't do too badly. For one thing, there were lots of places to hide; best of all, they seemed to be able to find a hot pool, which provided them with heating and cooking facilities. I think of my trip around Iceland when from the bus I could see the steam escaping from fissures in the earth, and the greenhouses erected over them. Over on the east side, where our tour bus guide grew up, he took us to a cave with a pair of hot pools in it, one for girls, one for boys, he said, where they swam and played (and washed?). I put my finger in the water; it was bath temperature. Even all those centuries ago, before the invention of electricity, Icelanders had those hot pools as a source of warmth. They were hungry, God knows, and when famine struck there was no denying starvation. But there are worse places to be than a sod house on a dark winter night, with other bodies, both animal and human, to keep you warm.

"Grub first, then ethics," said Bertold Brecht, but maybe also, "warmth first, then thought." Huddling in the dark is no joke, but while shadows engender fear and trembling, the shivers can be delicious, the goose bump kind caused by tales of ghosts and trolls and all the monsters lurking in the darkness, as well as blood-stirring sagas of the ancient ones. That's where those storytellers come in, not only keeping the dark at bay, but encouraging their listeners to warm their hands and minds over the flame of creation,

---

4 *Adventures, Outlaws and Past Events, Icelandic Folktales III*, translated by Alan Boucher, Reykjavik: *Iceland Review Library* , third printing, 1981.

reminding them of who they are and where they came from. Without story there is no thought, only uncharted feelings; no springboard of discovery, only inchoate reactions; in short, no sense of identity.

I once interviewed a man who was dying of bone cancer. He was in constant pain, except, he said, when he was speaking, delivering a sermon. He told me that the pain lifted then. As long as he was thinking and talking, the pain lay above his head. When he stopped, it returned. "The pain is always there," he said, "waiting for me." But you see, Helga, he could lift it when he focused on something else. So, in the darkness, hungry but perhaps not so terribly cold—our ancestors lifted their pain to a shining height.

I tried to say something of this to Sigriður Sigurðardóttir as we lingered over hot chocolate on our return to the present. It is my personally idiosyncratic theory that the tales we tell in the darkness of our long winter nights have the most meaning for us. This is when we expose our fears, share them, and perhaps lay them to rest, or at least, ease them as we tell each other how to endure. For northern people these stories began with the sagas—the first literature in Europe, written in the vernacular, rather than Latin; preserved on vellum, to last; and bound in scarce wood, recording the oral traditions of previous centuries. Those tales, a combination of family trees and feats of derring-do, stories of blood-feuds and conquests—adventures and exploits as gory as any present-day Terminator legend—those tales seem to answer some of our questions: *Where did I come from? What am I doing here?* and not only *Who am I?* but *How shall I live?* Our roots and our meaning, our dreams and our aspirations, our art and our identity come from tales told in the dark.

So, Helga, that's why I went back to Iceland, to confirm my theory of comfort and creation. We seek two kinds of comfort, I think, and those of us in Canada who try to ignore the one are in grave danger of mindless hedonism as we seek to satisfy the other. Now, I think, more than ever, it is important not only to our comfort but to our growth that we tell our stories. Comfort enables us to be secure within ourselves; we have established a connection with a "ground of being" on which we can rest. Growth indicates that the ground is fertile. From the darkness where the roots are we can seek light.

Come. Come and sit in the dark with me and let us tell stories.

— NOT QUITE KIN, BUT YOUR FRIEND BETTY JANE

CHAPTER EIGHT

SNORRI AND THE EDDAS
—LETTER TO WESTERN ICELANDERS

DEAR FRIENDS:

We meet every year at Thorrablót, and sometimes at Islendingadagurinn, so we must have some kind of connection with Iceland and things Icelandic. However, I suspect that if you're a diluted Western Icelander like me, you probably know more about *vínar terta* than you do about Snorri Sturluson, the Eddas and the sagas. What has happened to us has happened to successive generations of other immigrants: they are absorbed into their adopted country and they lose the language, the culture and the stories. It's only natural. Does it matter?

Considering the odds on the survival of the ones who made it possible for us to be here at all, and considering the astonishing culture from which we came, I think it does. I'm not going to give you any huge lecture, but I want to share with you my discoveries about our heritage, if only to enable you to tell better bedtime stories to your children and grandchildren.

Snorri Sturluson stands like a giant with his awesome contribution to Icelandic literature. Born in 1178 (or maybe 1179; birth records were a little sketchy in those days), he grew up in a foster home from the age of three where he acquired a deep grounding in and broad understanding of Icelandic/Norse tradition. His foster father was Jon Loptsson, perhaps the most powerful chieftain in Iceland, an ordained priest and avid historian, grandson of

Saemundur Sigfusson the Wise, the first recognized Icelandic historian. When Snorri was 20 he married Hallveig Ormsdóttir, a widow who happened to be the richest heiress in Iceland, not a bad start to acquiring his own wealth. He settled at Reykholt, where it is thought that he wrote most of his work, between 1223 and 1235. By that time he was already active in political affairs.

He was twice "lawspeaker" of the Alþing: from 1215 to 1218 and from 1222 to 1232. Perhaps he overestimated his own influence. When he travelled to Norway in 1218, he talked King Haakon into letting him try to become king of Iceland and win the Icelanders over to Haakon's side.[1] Acknowledging Haakon as his king and giving the Norwegian king his son as hostage, Snorri returned to Iceland in 1220. When Snorri failed in his intrigue, Haakon stirred up a feud between him and his kinsman Sturla. Being lawspeaker again didn't help much. Snorri was outlawed and fled to Norway in 1237. Then, in 1239, against Haakon's wishes, he returned to Iceland and was, on the king's command, murdered at Reykholt by his son-in-law, Gissur Thorvaldsson, in 1241.

The story goes that Snorri tried to escape through a secret underground tunnel, but didn't succeed. When I was at Reykholt I saw the Snorrlaug, Snorri's own private hot pool, which I was told connected to the house by an underground passage. I guess that's what he used to try to get away. Standing on the edge of that pool today is like standing on the edge of history—closest thing to a time machine I've ever experienced, outside of Glaumbær.

Snorri was a descendant of the poet Egill Skallagrimsson, hero of *Egils Saga;* some even attribute that saga to Snorri. Not necessary. His works, *Edda* and *Heimskringla,* put

---

1 Apparently it was internal feuds like this that led to full submission to the King of Norway by 1262, with a new monarchical code of government (1271). Norway and Denmark formed the Kalmar Union in 1397, at which time Iceland came under the control of the King of Denmark.

him in the ranks of the world's greatest authors. Call him the Icelandic Shakespeare and be grateful that such a giant lived. The *Snorra-Edda* is sometimes called the *Younger Edda* or the *Prose Edda*, to keep it separate in people's minds from the older, *Poetic Edda.*

The *Poetic Edda,* also known as the *Elder Edda*, is a collection of more than 30 poems about Scandinavian and Norse gods and human heroes. The stories were written down more than a thousand years ago. The *Elder Edda is* actually more Germanic than Icelandic, but the language (Old Norse) is now inaccessible (without a translation) to anyone but the Icelanders.

There's a new online e-zine, *Utgarð*,[2] "a magazine of the Northern tradition," which in its second issue in June 1998 featured a major piece about Eddic and Skaldic poetry with detailed instructions for writing your own. It seems that some of our contemporaries are just as interested in composing their own Skaldic poetry as they are in cooking *fiskabollur*. Skaldic, by the way, pertains to *skald*, a word for poet in both English and Icelandic. It comes from the Old Norse *skald* (the *a* is pronounced *o*)—a poet, narrator, especially a satirist, and so we get our modern word *scold*— "a person given to faultfinding."

Eddic verse usually deals with mythology and heroes; skaldic verse usually pays tribute to a lord or king. Skaldic verse follows very strict formal rules of metre; eddic verse is much simpler both in language and in metre. Aside from the distinctive and complicated rhythms and metre, which I won't go into, there are two major characteristics of all of this Norse poetry: alliteration, that is, the same sound being used at the beginning of successive words for emphasis; and kennings, a riddling paraphrase of a word whose meaning may now be lost to us, making the allusion rather hard to understand.

---

2 http://www.skergard.org/U2eddic.htm

Auden translated a collection of *Norse Poems*[3] and offers a glossary at the front of the book with a collection of phrases, mostly kennings. Here are a few examples: "Aegir's daughters" means waves; "din-world" is the mortal world of pain; "elf-candle" is the sun; "tree-foe" is fire. Thus, if we don't know, for example, that the giant Aegir was the Scandinavian lord of the sea, we would have no idea that "Aegir's daughters" means waves. "Skald-craft" was a hugely complicated form of poetry and demanded a deep knowledge of Norse mythology as well as an inspired use of language.

At its most complex, a kenning is both metaphor and metonymy: the use of the part for the reference to the whole (hands for workers; swords for soldiers). Kenning is said to come from an Old Icelandic verb meaning "to name after," but I think it has more to do with recognition, as in the song, "Do ye *ken* John Peel?"

I first came across kennings when I studied Anglo-Saxon poetry: the epic poem *Beowulf*, and the few extant poems and fragments. I still remember a kenning for snow— "coldest of corn"—and think of it whenever the weather produces that terrible hard snow that's more like hail than snowflakes. I notice that television weather reports refer to "snow grains" and skiers check out "corn snow." The name Beowulf is a kenning, I just learned, from "bee," associated with honey, and "wolf," which was synonymous with thief in the Norse mind; a "honey-thief" was a bear. This bear called Beowulf—and, yes, he was a big man, "with 30 men's strength in his grasp," was also called, as many heroes were, a "wielder of swords" and his lord and king was called a "giver of rings." I used to think that meant finger-rings, but they were arm-rings, much bigger and more valuable, also easier to divide—just hack them in half with an axe.

3 W.H. Auden & Paul B. Taylor, London: Faber & Faber, 1983.

The two best-known and most-important poems in the *Poetic Edda* are *Voluspá,* "The Prophecy of the Seeress" or "The Song of the Sibyl," and *Hávamál,* "The Words of the High One," in which the Norse god Oðin, the High One, drops words of wisdom learned while hanging on a branch of the World Tree. (He is said to have learned to cast runes while he was up there, too—not an easy thing to do.) *Hávamál* is a sequence of six poems, featuring two voices: a kind of master of ceremonies or guide, and the speaker, whose voice is supposed to be Odin's. The first of these poems is often called the *Gestathattr,* the guests' section. It begins with advice to a traveller who stays with strangers, a combination of a handbook for Vikings and Miss Manners's rules for visitors. It has been compared with the aphorisms of Confucius or Lao Tse. Among the few inexpensive souvenirs it is possible to buy in Iceland are small books of aphorisms from the *Hávamál.* Almost all the advice applies as well today as it did in the 11th century, except perhaps this one: "Never walk away from home ahead of your axe and sword." You wouldn't get far carrying an axe and sword today.

When W.H. Auden returned to Iceland for a second look in 1965, he pursued an interest he'd had from his early days at Oxford University when he read Norse mythology. He subsequently collaborated with a translator, Paul B. Taylor, on an English version of 13th-century (or earlier) Icelandic poetry, using the strong stresses of the Icelandic lines, as well as alliteration and kennings. *Norse Poems* was published posthumously in 1981 (Auden died in 1973), with careful completion by Taylor.[4] Perhaps it won't surprise you to learn that "The Words of the High One" *(Hávamál)* and "The Song of the Sibyl" *(Voluspá)* are included in this collection. I cannot resist including a few

---

4 *The Edda* by Auden and the same translator has also been published posthumously.

of the aphorisms in Auden's words, succinct and memorable. Here are some of my favourites, from the High One:

> *Who travels widely needs his wits about him,*
> *The stupid should stay at home.*

> *He starts to stink who outstays his welcome*
> *In a hall that is not his own.*[5]

> *Be not over-wary, but wary enough,*
> *First, of the foaming ale,*
> *Second, of a woman wed to another,*
> *Third, of the tricks of thieves.*

Auden has a way with words, even ones that are not originally his. One more:

> *Never rise at night unless you need to spy*
> *Or to ease yourself in the outhouse.*

Now, how about the *Voluspá? Völva* is Icelandic for sibyl. A web site[6] offers some comments about *Voluspá* written by kids. Here's an example: "One of the best known of the mythological lays is *Voluspá.*" (I don't think the sibyl would have appreciated that recommendation.) *Völva,* the personified seer, describes the events of history, both past and future, painting a clear picture of the pagan world. Here are some more reactions from the young reviewers:

The poem is about the history of the world from the beginning of it to the end and also about what happens after the end. My personal opinion is that the poem is rather boring,

---

5 This idea was first attributed to the Latin poet Horace, who said that guests, like fish, stink after three days.
6 I offer grateful acknowledgement to the creators at
http://rvik.ismennt.is/~harpa/form/ml_eng/edda/evolva.htm, now defunct.

it does not suit my line of interest.
    —Written by Orvar Olafsson.

Voluspá is based on how the *Völva* predicts what the end of
the world will be, how everything will crumble, burn and
shake under everyone's feet, but the world will become
beautiful again afterwards. She blames everyone for what
is to happen. You might think that it would be her fault
because it is incredible how she might know the turn of
events so accurately.
    —Written by Solrun Halla.

It does not say in any source who the *Völva* really is or where
she comes from. I don't think she is a god like in Christianity.
You don't need to know who she is because she is so noble.
I would rather think of her as a storyteller, because someone
had to exist to tell about how the world was created.
Present day fortune tellers have to this day not come close to
telling as good information as the *Völva* does. She is the *Völva*
of *Völvas*. Present day *Völvas* are fortune tellers that publish in
the magazines. They very often tell what will happen next
year. Our *Völva* tells about the end of the world in detail and
she doesn't publish in a magazine, she talks to O∂in himself.
    —Written by Aesa, Sigurbjorg, and Dagbjort.

Oh, the *Völva* of *Völvas*! What I like about these comments is that they prove the *Poetic Edda* is alive and vital
and still being read critically by young people today.

The *Snorra-Edda,* the work of one man, Snorri Sturluson,
is poetic, though it's called the *Prose Edda*. It is, in fact, like
a handbook for poets, concentrating on *dróttkvædi* (in
English best translated as Skaldic poetry), the old verse
form, dating from pagan times. It was Snorri's answer to the
court poetry that he had been exposed to in Norway and
that he feared, with some justification, would supersede
the old genre. Njördur P. Njardvík, a professor of Icelandic
literature at the University of Iceland, says that if Snorri

hadn't written his *Edda*, "the world of the ancient skaldic poetry would be hidden from us and our knowledge of Norse mythology as a whole would be very limited."[7] "Limited" is Nordic understatement. Almost everything we know about Norse mythology comes from the two *Edda*s.

The *Prose Edda* is composed of four sections:

1) The Prologue.
2) The Delusion of Gylfi, a sort of question-and-answer piece whereby, in spite of efforts to delude him, the wise king Gylfi learns the basics of Norse mythology and tells all.
3) *Skáldskaparmál,* or Poetic Diction, about skaldic metaphors.
4) Types of Metre.

Scholars inform us that Snorri wrote the last section first. Aside from the fact that it is a long, rather tedious eulogy to King Haakon, it's remarkable because it's written in 100 different metres, with asides setting out rules for alliteration, internal rhymes, long and short syllables, and the number of syllables in each line.

The section called *Skáldskaparmál* deals with two aspects of skaldic poetry: *heiti* and *kenningar*—kennings. *Heiti* are rare words, what we would call poetic diction, perhaps, like "ere" and "ope"—the kind of self-consciously poetic (read: obsolete) words that are so popular today in crossword puzzles. There were hundreds of *heiti* in the old skaldic poetry and Snorri lists them all, very Icelandic of him.

The other work by Snorri is *Heimskringla*, an exhaustive history of the Norwegian kings, the title taken from the beginning of the piece: "*Kringla heimsins*" ("the orb of the world"). Centuries later this would be the name of an Icelandic newspaper established in Winnipeg in 1886. It

---

7 From an essay in *Icelandic Times* magazine, "Celebrating Snorri: Creator of Documentary Fiction."

survives today in a double name as it amalgamated with *Lögberg* (which means "law rock," an actual place at Thingvellir), the other local newspaper, founded in 1888. Since 1959, *Lögberg-Heimskringla*, with a circulation of 1,000, has been published weekly. (I have a subscription.) I'm not sure many Western Icelanders, even ones who speak Icelandic, know that their weekly newspaper derives its name from Snorri Sturluson's history book.

Njördur Njardvík comments that the most amazing quality of Snorri's work is its narrative technique. It is, he says, a "fusion of history and fiction," what we would call today creative non-fiction. In the confident manner of later writers, Snorri does not hesitate to put words in people's mouths, as if he'd had a tape recorder or as if they hadn't been dead for a couple of centuries. He weaves history with character development, creating a seamless whole. His technique had an enormous influence on the ensuing Icelandic sagas, which are full of dialogue. His voice has been heard across the centuries.

Like many of us in the Western world, I cut my baby teeth on Greek and Roman mythology. These days, kids probably know more about Frodo and Bilbo, or the Ninja Turtles, than Bacchus or Aphrodite. The point is that I didn't know much about Norse mythology, just a few of the names, like Thor, the god of war, who swung a mean hammer, and Freya, the beautiful spinner. The best-known story from the sagas was probably the Volsunga Saga, which Richard Wagner used as a base for his Ring Cycle. I remember looking at pictures in *The Book of Knowledge* showing the Valkyries, a dozen winged women warriors, who swooped down over battlefields and picked up slain heroes to take them to Valhalla, which wasn't quite heaven, but a nice place where fallen fighters were honoured (a fête better than death?). And then there was the hero, Sigurd, who strode through a ring of fire to rescue Brunhilde.

It wasn't until relatively late in life that I read a presentation of Greek, Roman and Norse mythology by Edith Hamilton.[8] There are seven main sections to the book; only a skimpy Part Seven deals with the Norse stories, but they had a profound effect on me. I began to read the sagas. They are astonishing; the oldest literature in Europe, a record of the lives and deaths of ordinary people, with enough details to lure the reader into all kinds of theories and suppositions. They led me to further speculation about the people who told and eventually wrote down those tales. I began to wonder, how could they do it? With their eyes wide shut, nightowls tell stories.

—FROM A DAUGHTER OF FREYA, BETTY JANE WYLIE

---

8 *Mythology*, by Edith Hamilton. New York: The Universal Library, Grosset & Dunlap, A Little, Brown & Company Edition, 1942.

CHAPTER NINE

LANGUAGE
—LETTER TO MY COUSIN'S GRANDSON

DEAR KOL:

It is entirely fitting that I address this letter to you, as the fifth-generation male Tergesen in Canada. I know you don't speak Icelandic, which bears out my contention that although culturally attuned to Iceland, we Western Icelanders have lost the language. Therefore, it will not be amiss for me to consider the matter of language with you. You may not appreciate it now, but your *amma* (my cousin Lorna) will. Our heritage is rich and poetic, the only classical language left in the modern world—and therefore difficult for people to learn.

The verbs conjugate and the nouns decline, that is, they change form according to the number (singular or plural) they refer to and to what part of speech they play in a sentence. Articles are not separate; they are attached to the end of nouns, indicating number and form. Two or more words can be telescoped together to make a new word like Lewis Carroll's "portmanteau" words. Because the Icelanders have been so isolated over the centuries and therefore not subject to the influences of other languages, Icelandic has remained very pure. That's why Icelanders today can read Old Norse without a translation. They are very conscious and proud of this fact and work at maintaining the language of which they are inordinately fond.

The watchdog, the Icelandic Language Institute, is more purist about preserving the language than the famous

Académie Française is about keeping French free of foreign influences. Anglicisms have infiltrated French *(le nightclub, le hot dog)* but Icelandic will have none of them, eschewing even the use of Greek and Roman roots to describe modern concepts and inventions. I first noticed this on the public signs outside of telephone booths; the signs read *SIMI*. Not a hint of the Greek root that we use— *tele*—indicating distance. *Simi* comes from the word *seima*, meaning to sew; *simi* is the thread, the line, the connection between two phones. "You can say everything in Icelandic," says Kristján Árnason, professor of Icelandic at the University of Iceland. "You don't need English to express yourself."

The purists seek legitimate Icelandic words with impeccable history. Thus, television is *sjónvarp,* from *sjón,* meaning view; *varp,* from a verb root meaning cast or throw—a thrown view or picture. Auden thought the word for bicycle was *foss,* because it went as fast as a waterfall; someone had told him that. I looked up the word in my English/Icelandic dictionary. It's *hjólhestur,* and it translates as a wheel-horse; tricycle is *þríhjól*—a three-wheeler.

When I went to search out the word for computer, I thought I might be on to something when I saw that the word that sounds like reckon *(reikna)* means compute, but that's only accounting or calculating. A computer, of course, does much more than that. The word in Icelandic is *tölva* and the roots are marvellous: *tá,* meaning digit or finger and *völva,* meaning sibyl. Remember *Voluspá,* ("The Song of the Sibyl"), the *Völva* of all *Völvas?* Could anything be more fitting than that the *Völva,* the seer who has a direct line with Oðin, be invoked for a 20th-century miracle? And so Icelandic gives us a finger-wizard, a digital sibyl, pointing the way to a future in cyberspace.

As I write, Icelandic computer operators are having a battle with Microsoft. Although the country is computerized, ranking 17th among the countries of the world for its

Internet usage, the population is so small that the number is still small potatoes to Bill Gates, who refused to translate Windows 95 into Icelandic for them, although it is available in Slovenian and Catalan. Gates knows that every Icelandic schoolchild learns English; why bother translating? This worries Icelandic educators. Schoolchildren start early on PCs; 96 percent of Icelandic schools are on the Internet. Professor Árnason thinks they are in danger, because, he says, "The language of computers soon becomes the language of the kitchen."

Iceland's minister of culture has appealed directly to Microsoft headquarters, saying that if Iceland doesn't get a Microsoft translation, other means will be found of computerizing the schools. A vague promise to translate Windows 98 has been held out, but nothing has come of it so far. Is the writing on the screen? This brings up my favourite Icelandic old word for a new product. The word for the computer screen or monitor in Icelandic is *skjár,* a perfectly good word that people hadn't needed for several centuries, since they stopped using stretched cows' bladders[1] as windows in the sod houses. Now I can visualize the kind of light that filtered through into the *baðstofa.*

I found an entire Icelandic English glossary of geoscience terms on the Net,[2] published by an American scientist, Richard S. Williams, Jr., in a U.S. Geological Survey from the Quissett Campus, Woods Hole, Massachusetts. Williams explains what he refers to as the Icelandic characteristic of naming things with compound phrases (kennings). This method extends to placenames, too. He cites the volcanic island of Surtsey as a case in point, a lovely case and an intriguing point.

Surtsey emerged like Venus from the foam in 1963 when an undersea volcanic eruption thrust up a spanking new

---

1 Actually, I learned that it was not a cow's bladder but the amniotic sac of a calf that was used. My Glaumbær guidebook didn't get that technical.

2 http://woodshole.er.usgs.gov/epubs/rwilliams/geoicelandic.html

island southwest of the Westmann Islands off Reykjavik. It took three years to build up from the volcanic core, resulting, 950 feet above the ocean floor, in an island one square mile (2.5 kilometres) in area, with elevations of up to 560 feet (171 metres). This newest place on earth is a closely guarded, meticulously analyzed, living, breathing lab for eager scientists, who prize it as an eco-lab. Consider this, Kol: it was sterile, untouched by anything, when it arose. Any life form that invades it is news, whether it's seaweed or airborne seeds or birds just dropping by. I think it's the closest thing to a 20th-century Garden of Eden I ever heard of.

Anyway, the name *Surtsey* is a compound word put together from *ey,* the Icelandic word for island, and *Surts,* the possessive of *Surtur,* the fire god of Norse mythology. Legend has it that he was a world destroyer; in this case, he created one—Surtur's Island. I keep expecting the scientists to discover Adam and Eve hiding out in a cave on Surtsey.

Williams gives another example using another favourite of mine, *Snæfellsjökull,*[3] a glacier on the tip of the Snæfellsnes peninsula, west of Reykjavik. On a clear summer night you can see the sun set (briefly) over *Snæfellsjökull* at about two in the morning, according to my cousin Hebba and her husband, Hreggviður, who live on the east side of the city. Gazing across the harbour from their living-room windows, they watch the sun light up the ice as it slides briefly behind *Snæfellsjökull* before they go to bed. *Snær* is the Icelandic word for snow; *fells,* the possessive of a word for a mountain (think of the fells of Scotland, and while you're at it, note that *tjörn* is a small lake or pool and think of a Scottish tarn). *Jökull,* by the way, the Icelandic word for glacier, has the same origin as the English word for icicle.

---

3 It sounds as if you're sneezing when you say it.

Williams tries to ease his readers into the difficulties of reading scientific and technical words in Icelandic, going into considerable detail to explain the rather poetic way that Icelandic identifies its natural features and phenomena. He points out that the careful, conscious avoidance of loan words and roots from other languages, even when they have a scientific justification, make it difficult for a scientist accustomed to an almost universal language. Williams concludes, "in addition to the challenge of learning Icelandic, the serious student of the geoscience literature of Iceland is faced with also learning a specialized scientific vocabulary with few cognates." Twenty pages of glossary follow in four columns showing the singular form of the word in question; the plural; the class/gender and the English meaning. It's fascinating.

The geothermal system of heat distribution is *hitaveita*, simply hot water. Terminal moraine, the detritus of a glacier, is *jökulgarðar,* which translates literally into glacier garden—much prettier! And here's a nice one: a meteorite is a *loftsteinn*, a sky stone.

Just to corroborate what I have already reported to others about Reykjavik, the capital city: *reykur* means smoke or steam (are you familiar with the Scottish expression *"lang may your lum reek,"* meaning, "long may your chimney smoke"?), and *vík* is bay. Thus, the name Reykjavik is itself, like these other examples, a kenning, a compound phrase describing a thing in poetic terms. Modern Icelandic tends to use kennings when it needs new words for new things. We're back to poetry!

Now I want to say a little about the building blocks of the language—of English, too. The Indo-European language base is the source of about half the world's languages.[4] The metaphor of the Tower of Babel in the

---

4 Some of the following information is condensed and adapted from *The 1999 Canadian Encyclopedia: World Edition,* by McClelland & Stewart Inc., 1988. My other source is my notebook from my university course in Anglo-Saxon.

Old Testament illustrates quite simply and vividly the dispersal of language into disparate tongues, which is what happened as the various speakers lost contact and broke into a variety of speech forms, grammar, diction, and so on. Some similarities, that is, roots, are still possible to trace, usually to do with numbers, body parts and kinship. Speech came first, then symbols; written forms varied as well, ranging from cuneiform, hieroglyphics and a variety of alphabets, some of which retained some similarity to each other.[5]

What concerns me here are the subfamilies and the subgroups that led to the language you and I speak today and the other one that I wish I could. Both English and Icelandic derive from a Germanic subfamily: Old Norse and Icelandic (which includes Danish, Faeroese, Norwegian and Swedish) from North Germanic. English worked its way to us from the West Germanic, through Low German (Afrikaans, Dutch, Flemish, Frisian). Latin and Classical Greek, of course, each went in different directions, and then Latin sailed in on top of Old English via the Roman conquerors, which is why modern English has different-sounding words for the same things.

Equations have been worked out to track the sound shifts or consonant shifts through the Germanic groups. Grimm's Law, named after the Grimm brothers who did all the research on fairy tales, provides us with a guide to the consistent pattern of the change—two, actually.

The first goes like this: *p, d, t* and *k* in Latin, Greek and Sanskrit become *f, th,* and *h* in the Germanic. So, Latin *pater* becomes English *father;* Latin *pisces* becomes English *fish;* Latin *dent,* English *tooth;* Latin *cornu,* English *horn.* Later the conquerors brought us *paternal, piscatorial* and *dentist,* and *cornucopia,* so we inherited a plethora of words.

---

5 I once managed to find my way through the Russian subway system by pronouncing the station names phonetically, based on my knowledge of the Greek alphabet, which bears some likeness to the Cyrillic alphabet.

Those sound shifts were already occurring between the 7th and 9th centuries. In addition, before the 8th century, a second shift slipped into some of the West German dialects, but not always. Sometimes *d* became *t* and the *t* became *ss* or *z* (English *bread,* German *Brot;* English foot, German *Fuss;* English *ten,* German *zehn*). I find it continually interesting to explore the origins of words. I hope you will, too, as you grow older, Kol.

Icelandic, which derives from the North Germanic, and which does not have a Roman overlay of vocabulary to absorb, retained a closer connection with Old Norse, obviously, than English did with its grandmother, Old English. The one thing that Iceland was invaded by was the Roman alphabet, which was introduced at the same time as Christianity, about A.D. 1000. Before that, there were runes.

The Viking alphabet, known as the *Fuþark*, comprised 23 letters or runes, all of them formed of straight lines because they could be more easily carved in wood or stone than curves. The good news for posterity is that the Roman alphabet was established before Snorri Sturluson began to write. All the sagas are accessible to us because of that alphabet. Modern Icelandic still uses it along with three extra letters: the "thorn" which looks like this—þ—and sounds like *th* in think; the "eth" which looks like this—ð—and sounds like *th* in mother. Then there's the diphthong *æ*, found in several European languages, which sounds like the a-sound in "ash," plus an umlaut with *o* to make it a separate letter that looks like this—ö—and sounds like *oh*. Icelandic also uses diacritics: acute accents over the vowels and the *y* to indicate the pronunciation. Bill Gates should pay attention, but you don't have to, Kol, unless you decide to learn to read and write Icelandic. Then you'll have to work at it.

I'm happy to tell you that at least my Microsoft program includes these letters and accents in a "Character Map" so that I can add them to my manuscript. The net offers a few different web address (URLs or Uniform Resource Locators) for "Icelandicizing" one's computer and it is possible to buy software which includes these fonts. It's amazing what can be found on a *skjár!*

W. H. Auden had a way of recognizing a real poet; he said if he [she?] likes "hanging around words listening to what they have to say," he must be a poet. I would say, if you are besottedly in love with words, you're probably a poet, and maybe even an Icelander. A love of language seems to go with the territory. In the old days, I am told, all Icelanders were poets. In his novel, *Independent People*, Halldór Laxness tells of his character Bjartur keeping himself alive during a blizzard by reciting every piece of poetry he has ever read, heard or composed himself. Poetry was more than a pastime; it helped him make it through the night.

In *Letters to Iceland*, Auden reported that the rhyming gene was still active. He described a playful habit people enjoyed when they met on the road: one walker would declaim an extemporaneous, relevant poem, to be greeted by the other "half," equally spontaneous and matching the first in rhyme scheme and rhythm. Auden said that Icelanders could create entire palindromic poems (reading the same backwards as forwards, as in "Madam, I'm Adam") going on for several lines. Maybe the language with its different endings and inflexions helped them, but not that much.

I think that games like that arose as surely as the sagas out of the endless, dark nights of an Icelandic winter. Those first decades in Canada would have done nothing to dispel the habit. Almost equally endless nights and even harsher winters must have continued to force poetry as pastime from icebound, restless minds.

---

6 Published by Canadian Museum of Civilization, Hull, 1992, a companion volume to *Icelandic-Canadian Oral Narratives*, 1991.

Magnús Einarsson's delightful book of *Icelandic-Canadian Memory Lore*[6] is chock-full of rhymes: lullabies and prayers, riddles, rigmaroles (lists) and games, playful poems and scary songs, drinking chants, dances and reels, narrative poems, proverbs and sayings in playful, mnemonic verses, all from "authors" in New Iceland. Some of the material is for children; some is adult entertainment and prayers; the proverbs may be considered lore, wisdom to be passed down, some strangely reminiscent of the *Hávamál,* but with a new country's spin in a different environment. I can't resist a few examples:

The rooster is bravest on his own dunghill.

Householding is difficult,
marriage is a misery,
the single life is bad,
and something is wrong with all of them.

A detour is better than a bog.

A man without a book is blind.

This rich material flows from the recorded memories of immigrant Icelanders and their families, passed down in Icelandic. (The book is bilingual, Icelandic and English.) These recollections seem to indicate that the penchant for poetry still survives through the Western Icelandic mind, though it may be weakening now with the attrition of the original language. Magnús is not too down-hearted about what he calls the "demise of an active Icelandic culture in North America." He points out that it's not the end of the story because "the culture of the immigrant generation and their children has given rise to a uniquely Icelandic-Canadian culture." We're still here, aren't we?

—YOUR FIRST COUSIN TWICE REMOVED, BEEJAY

CHAPTER TEN

THE SAGAS
—LETTER TO MY GRANDSON

DEAR WILLIAM:

I am addressing this letter about the sagas to you not only because you are my first born grandchild, son of my son, but also because you have already (at the age of 15) expressed an interest in writing. This is where it all begins, in narrative.

I've been reading the sagas,[1] fascinated by these blood-thirsty, pragmatic tales, trying to see if there's any relationship between me and our family and those brooding, humor-ous ruffians who apparently created poetry as readily as they initiated a blood feud, and who took both equally seri-ously. W.H. Auden has commented that the old Vikings demonstrated the "gangster virtues," and in many ways this is true. Just think of the infamous St. Valentine's Day Massacre. The tale of the gangsters' murders would write up quite well as a saga. So far I feel a greater affinity with elves and trolls than I do with an Icelandic Mafia.

But if they were only about bloodletting, the sagas would not have had the enormous impact on European literature that they did. Apart from the miracle of their existence—their having been written in the first place—which in itself is staggering, there is the depth and breadth and sheer volume of these most collective of works, set down by anonymous writers during the 13th and 14th centuries, several hundred

---

1 Paperback copies of translations by different people, by various publishers. Most of the sagas are now available on the Net, in public domain. Just look up the name of the saga you want to read, and you get it chapter by chapter.

years after the events they describe. Embellished and enlarged in the best oral traditions, they were already a kind of miracle when they were recorded not in Latin, but in the native vernacular—the biggest miracle of all.

That's too sweeping a description of a literature that spanned a couple of centuries. The events that inspired the stories took place from about 930, when the first settlement was established, to about 1050, but they weren't written down until early in the 12th century when the Book of Settlements *(Landnámabók)* was compiled. It's an account, mostly genealogical, of the first settlers, the people who came from the western districts of Norway to Iceland along with a few of their Celtic thralls (servants, closer to slaves). It was these people who, adopting a code of law based on the laws of the Norwegian *Gulaþing,* set up a state with four Quarters, each with a chieftain in charge; they also established the two-week annual assembly of the whole nation, the Alþing, when disputes were heard and judgements were handed down. In spite of the bloody feuds described in some of the sagas, this system of government lasted for nearly three and a half centuries, so they must have been, on the whole, fairly peaceful. Partly because of this stability the great Icelandic culture developed, producing a literature unmatched in Europe during that time.

The Book of Settlements listed some 430 original settlers, both male and female, naming their lines of descent, and reporting on their homesteads and boundaries. What began as a piece of factual scholarship was embroidered with anecdotes and folk tales that turned it into a kind of literature as opposed to straight history. That was just the beginning.

Most of the sagas were actually written down between 1190 and 1320. They fall into three main classifications. First, there were the Kings' Sagas, which told the stories of

the rulers of Scandinavia, still home to the Icelandic settlers. Of these, the best-known is the *Heimskringla* by Snorri
Sturluson, which tracks the Norwegian kings from their
descent from Oðin down to Magnús Erlingsson (1184). Next
came the Icelanders' Sagas, about the great families who
lived in Iceland from 930 to 1030. Their creators, that is,
the people who finally set these stories down, are unknown,
but their achievement is considered to be the best of the
golden age of Icelandic writing. They include the stories
of Egill, Gisli the outlaw, Njáll, Grettir, and the people of
Laxárdal, with a great woman—Guðrun Ósvifsdóttir—as
the central character. After the Icelanders' Sagas there were
the legendary sagas, which were essentially romances, por-
traying a more idealized picture of olden times and largely
influenced by French romance literature.

Recently the major sagas have been made available to a
wider reading public, in a boxed set of five beautifully
bound volumes. Claiming some notable firsts—first time
in English (that is, the complete set), first time coordinat-
ed—*The Complete Sagas of Icelanders* has been published
in Reykjavik by Leifur Eiríksson Publishing Company. The
editors, Viðar Hreinsson (General Editor), Robert Cook,
Terry Gunnell, Keneva Kunz and Bernard Scudder, inform
us that this edition is the first English translation of the
entire body of the sagas of Icelanders, 40 in all, along with
the 49 tales connected with them. Supporting material
includes maps and tables, notes on the poetic imagery,
illustrations and diagrams, a glossary and an index of characters—some 700 people from a cast of thousands, chosen
for their appearance in two or more of the sagas. Before I
die, William, I want to own and read this collection.

Icelanders can read their heritage at will. As I have said,
the language has changed so little over the centuries that
a modern Icelander can read Old Norse without a translation. Try offering *Beowulf* to English scholars today and

see if they can read it without an Anglo-Saxon dictionary. Even Chaucer's Middle English is slow going for most English academics. For that matter, Shakespeare's English presents a challenge to the average English theatregoing audience, one reason, perhaps, for the very broad interpretations, business and horseplay that directors and actors seem to find necessary.

Snorri Sturluson is credited with the style of the sagas, the laconic telling of the tale with no psychological interpretation, no report of people's feelings, except what they say themselves. You must surmise the presence of strong emotions and reactions from characters' behaviour, with this exception: Icelanders do not wallow. The conventional rule seems to be, if characters in a saga wish to express emotion, they have to do it in a poem. By the very discipline of this formal expression, they achieve distance from their audience, who must then guess the strength of their passion. So we get a straight, exciting narrative unbroken by introspective soul-searching, punctuated now and then by a poem. Did the Vikings have souls to search? Did they have any concept of self as we know it today? Probably not, at least, it had no name.

In *A History of Private Life, Volume III*[2] in his essay, "The Practical Impact of Writing," Roger Chartier suggests that the "privatization" of reading was one of the significant influences of the early modern era. The idea of self didn't emerge until after the invention of the printing press in Europe. Literacy and the increasing availability of books led to the luxury of reading to one's self. At first reading was a public act, when a literate storyteller read to a group from a book, itself a rare possession. When an individual began to read to himself, he had to read out loud, because he was accustomed to hearing the words. As reading

---

2 *A History of Private Life, Volume III: Passions of the Renaissance.* Roger Chartier, editor; Arthur Goldhammer, translator. Cambridge, MA and London, England: The Belknap Press of Harvard University Press, 1989.

became a private act, it became possible for him to develop thoughts about what he read, paving the way, as Chartier says, for "previously unthinkable audacities." (I use the masculine pronoun deliberately, because so few women were permitted to be literate at the time.) I believe that only then did people become *self*-conscious; and only after that did *self* evolve as a concept, from a defining prefix to an actual entity.

Does this mean that people had no self to speak of before they could read and think to themselves, by themselves? I'm sure they had, but I think there was a more direct route from action to reaction. Perhaps instead of an equation like *I think, therefore I am,* the logic was simpler: *I do, therefore I am*. I also believe that the reactions were not simply knee-jerk, that a great deal of conscious will was involved.

The people in the sagas are able to acknowledge pain—emotional suffering—in sophisticated ways. In the saga *A Tale from the Eastfirths*, in "The Tale of Gunnar Þriðandi's Bane," a man called Eyolf says to his enemy, "I would that I might one day tell you a tale that will give you no less pain than this, when you told me my brother was dead." This indicates not only the emotions the protagonist feels, but also shows his understanding that others, too, have felt similar anguish. The awareness of Other is what we might call modern, if that doesn't sound condescending.

The writers and their subjects existed in a bleak, harsh world with little promise of reward either on this earth or in a hereafter which didn't hold out much hope for anyone, except maybe for the slain non-Christian warriors the Valkyries carried to Valhalla. One had to rely on oneself (if not one's self) not to make a mess of things. The important thing was to do what one had to do, perform well and endure. The only thing that lived on after death was a man's (person's) good name, so he had better behave well to ensure that at least. As for the outcome, it was up to fate. If death was inevitable, no one was going to go down without a struggle and that struggle had to be courageous. These are pagan virtues we're talking about. Although these sagas were written down after Iceland had adopted Christianity officially, they referred to a time before it had arrived, and certainly before it had penetrated people's consciousness.

The tales are not only about battles, blood feuds, suffering and death; there are love stories as well, with people who die for love rather than for property. Here the women figure most prominently, not merely as the passive spoils, the reward for a man's conquest but also as movers in their own right, manipulating others to gain their own ends—a new love or a true love.

How do these stories go? Once upon a time, there was a man and his name was Soandso. He was from Suchandsuch a family from Some Dale and he had three brothers, and they were married and there were other relatives as well. He was big and strong and fair-haired, or he was a small man and cunning. He was rich and generous, or miserly; he was poor, but shared whatever he had with others. And so on. We get a thumbnail sketch of the hero and then we take off, swiftly moving into action, and what action! These people were often not only violent but also vicious.

I am not a violent person and I shudder at some of the horrible deaths the characters in the sagas meted out to their enemies. I suppose this behaviour is characteristic of early, barbaric societies everywhere (which makes it inexcusable in today's "enlightened" age?). On first reading, I found the viciousness and violence of the saga heroes hard to equate with the solid, stolid, laconic, phlegmatic, quiet (Western) Icelanders that I know. Our ancestors seemed to have no milk of human kindness running in their veins, not even goat's milk; more like ice water straight out of the glacier *Vatnajökull*. I have a theory for you to consider, William, that might help to explain the discrepancy between the violence of the Vikings and the stolid serenity of Icelanders today. The old ones killed each other off. Violence has been bred out of the race. Only the peaceful DNA has survived!

First, we have to understand the Icelanders' situation. As mentioned, the Alþing, the first law court or parliament in Europe, was established, in the first millennium. Once a year people gathered to set their affairs right, according to judgements passed by their peers, with a tribunal headed by the lawspeaker. Much as in the old city-states of Greece, such rulings were possible in a small, homogeneous society where everyone not only knew everyone else, but was related. The disputes were mainly about property and unfair business dealings: the dispersal of crops from shared land; grazing rights; who had the right to a beached whale; fishing rights (some things never change), and so on, with maybe a few disgruntled husbands or wives and bad marriages thrown in. Easy enough to present one's case, marshal arguments, get friends and family to vouch for one, and simple enough—sometimes— to get a ruling. The trick was how to enforce the ruling. There was no executive arm to the law.

Once the ruling was handed down, the plaintiff and defendant had to seek their own enforcement. If there was an argument or resistance, if the defendant disagreed with the judgement, he—or she—would go off and gather up family and friends to argue the decision. And then there'd be a fight, not only bloody and fatal, but also often cut-throat and devious. Of course, the following year there'd have to be another ruling. When a man became too violent or scheming or underhanded, he would be outlawed. That's what happened to Grettir the Strong, outlawed for 20 years. Most of the time such banishment worked. The outlaw would have to leave the country for a specified length of time. He stayed away on pain of death, a justified execution that could be carried out with legal impunity (although his immediate family might resent it, and take vengeance). And thereby hang these tales. They tell us how it was.

The Icelandic Sagas are based on family stories, as I have said. There are others, earlier, as also mentioned, like Snorri's tales of Norwegian kings, and later, what have been called contemporary and individual exploits. They were tales told over the years, tales told in the dark, tales about families, foes and heroes. They began as history and somewhere took a leap into the clean, bright light of narrative, forged in the heat of the narrator's eloquent passion and refined through the years. These stories, though set firmly into time and place, were condensed and polished, embroidered with invented details, embellished with strange and haunting events, and enlivened, yes, with gossip. Based on real-life chronological events, they were imbued with imagination until they were transformed into art. The people whose stories are told are, above all, human, with human frailties and emotions. They are not gods; they have no superhuman powers. Even the strongest among them have human weaknesses; Grettir the Strong, for all his heroic qualities and amazing strength, was afraid of the dark. He also had a terrible temper, which may have been the cause of his downfall.

He had an incompetent thrall, Glaum, who made dangerous errors—three of them—and the last one killed Grettir, as he had predicted it would when he berated old Glaum. Banished and hiding out on top of Drángey (Island), Grettir had enough problems without the hazards his servant presented. Glaum let the fire go out, and Grettir had to swim for more; that was one. Then Glaum dragged in a cursed piece of driftwood, a log that Grettir had rejected twice because he could sense it had a spell on it. Glaum brought it in because it was dark, the log was close and he was lazy; that was two. Cutting it angrily, Grettir slipped and gashed himself to the bone with his axe, resulting in a wound that would not heal. Sick as he was, unto death, he sent Glaum out to keep watch and Glaum did not bother to bring up the ladder by which visitors to the island were permitted to scale the cliff. That was the third big mistake. Grettir's enemies climbed the ladder, attacked the hideout and killed him. In the end, they killed old Glaum, too.

Writers past and present have been moved and influenced by the sweeping narrative and power of the sagas. In 1813, Scottish poet and novelist Sir Walter Scott expressed his fascination for *Eyrbyggja Saga,* his favourite. Commenting on the new publication of the Icelandic Sagas, American writer Kurt Vonnegut says: "Only now can I fully appreciate my own deep debt as a storyteller to Icelandic writers of long ago." The Czech novelist Milan Kundera tempers his praise with regret: "Although the glory of the sagas is indisputable, their literary influence would have been much greater if they had been written in the language of one of the major nations, and we would have regarded the sagas as an anticipation or even as the foundation of the European novel." I disagree. If another nation had attempted the task at the time the Icelanders did, the stories would have been written down in Latin, and what good would that have done? The very fact that they were recorded by a small nation in an obscure tongue actually preserved them for us.

The sagas are exciting, William, violent as I said, but also romantic and adventurous, eerie and even funny. You could do worse in your writing. It all begins with story.

—LOVE, AMMA

CHAPTER ELEVEN

THE NORSE MYTHS—A STORY
—LETTER TO MY UNCLE

DEAR UNCLE PETE:

This story is for you.

In the days following the accident that killed her husband, Kate dawdles her hours away, idling in memories. The casts have come off her arms. She squeezes rubber balls and twists her wrist 50 times a day to strengthen her grip and increase her flexibility. It still hurts to drive (and it scares her), but she can dress herself and cook, so her mother has left. She doesn't feel too alone when meal preparation and homework-checking keep her busy and reacting on a surface level, but when the children go to school each morning, silence and loneliness leave her helpless in the path of relentless, indiscriminate memories, relentless because she keeps reliving the moments of horror just before the truck hit them; indiscriminate because her mind keeps ranging back out of the way, into the past, somewhere, anywhere.

Are they indiscriminate?

One day Kate finds herself rereading a collection of sagas and remembering Svenn. He was no Viking hero.

As a child, when she was still Catherine with wide eyes and full of wonder, she had always been a little afraid of Uncle Svenn. For one thing, he smelled bad, reeked, in fact, some days, of tobacco and something else she didn't know for years was sour booze. His clothes, wrinkled and dusted with ash, hung on his thin, shaking body. Often unshaven and noisy (on bad days), he shambled and shouted on the streets. The higher the sun, the noisier he was. Later, as darkness fell, shadows subdued him.

He always lowered his voice and softened his face and nodded politely at young Catherine when he met her on the street, but he gave her the chance to ignore him. She always spoke first, said hello, called him by name, and he would mumble a reply. If the friends she was with—those who didn't already know—asked her who that was, she would reply clearly, "My uncle Svenn," as if defying them to say another word. They never did.

Other times, and looking back, Kate realizes these were more frequent, the child would see her uncle in the store, with a clean jaw and neat, pressed clothes, quietly helping a customer. Like the rest of the family, he was always quiet. Except when drunk. He spoke to Catherine even less in the sober times, acknowledging her greetings with an abrupt nod or grunt.

At the beginning of the summer, when she and her brother Dan and her mother moved into the cottage for two long, glorious months, Catherine would go the rounds dutifully to greet each relative. Svenn, like her other uncles, would give her a dollar but made no attempt to be jolly like Uncle Hans or Uncle Johann. Sometimes, though, he would give her a shy, crooked smile. When she was a little older and could reach Uncle Svenn's cheek without stretching on tiptoe, Catherine would peck him, like a small chicken scratching in the dirt.

Kate remembers that bristly cheek now, probably the second one she had experienced in her life. The child Catherine rarely saw her father's face stubbled like that, only when he had gone out in the night to deliver a baby and she had caught him before his morning ablutions— that's what he called them. It sounded clinical. As a little girl, she liked to stroke her father's cheeks after he had shaved, so smooth and fresh.

"All brave," she remembers saying to her father, and wonders what she meant. It sounded like a smooth word.

So it was some kind of ordeal Catherine set herself, to kiss Uncle Svenn's emery skin, proving with a gesture that she loved him. Did she? Proving that they were kin, anyway.

The three summers she lived with her grandmother and the people in the Big House, Catherine discovered less to love in her uncle. She learned her first Icelandic swear word from him; Kate still doesn't know what it means but assumes the worst and never says it. The child learned to go back to sleep when she woke up to hear Svenn roaring in the night and Amma's soothing tones shushing him, helping him as he stumbled noisily up the stairs, making sure he collapsed on the bed and not on the floor of his bedroom.

Catherine always walked by Uncle Svenn's bedroom very quickly, the last door on her way to the attic stairs. Usually the door was shut. When it was open, she could smell a crisp scent of peppermint or pine. Kate realizes now that Amma had her ways of masking the stink of whisky. The ashtrays were always clean every morning, and so were the sheets, but no one touched Uncle Svenn's papers, magazines or books. The papers and periodicals remained strewn on the floor but not the books, not the books, so carefully stored like jewels in a tall mahogany bookcase with hinged, glass-fronted doors to protect them from dust. They awed her grandmother. She never touched them. Catherine wanted to, but never did. Once she tiptoed into the room when Uncle Svenn was at the store, to see what kind of books he treasured, but she turned away disappointed when she discovered they were all printed in Icelandic.

Kate muses on them now. Still unable to speak, read or

write Icelandic and rueful at her deficiency, she wonders if she would have been able to talk to Svenn if she'd had that tongue. Not then; she was too young then. Later, she developed another language, a half a one, a kind of loose link, briefly, now gone. That was the year at the university, majoring in English, when she had studied Anglo-Saxon and translated *Beowulf*.

Kate had come to Gimli with her family to bury her grandmother in the dead of winter. She remembers the protest of the church bell as it rang, the clear tone of its ring followed by a dull thud as the frozen metal shuddered in the cold. She remembers Afi pulling his chair away from the table where the family was drinking coffee after the reception in the church. He took it over to the window and sat on it facing north, looking at a snow-covered yard, not seeing anything.

"It's so cold," he muttered. "She must be so cold out there."

"He's looking toward the cemetery," said Aunt Karin to the others.

Catherine, not so young anymore, watched him and thought she understood.

From then until his death Afi sat there, gazing in the direction of the cemetery, which lay north of the town.

Kate remembers the service held in the house before the funeral when the minister talked about her grandmother, evoking a life, speaking in Icelandic. She remembers understanding more than she had ever done in her life, only partly because the man spoke to her heart about someone she loved.

Later, after Afi had left his chair and gone upstairs, Catherine found herself alone at the kitchen table with Svenn. Her mother and father were in the den with the rest of the family, making plans. Kate's brother Dan had gone somewhere to read. He always went somewhere to read. Shyly, Kate told Svenn her discovery.

"I understood a little," she said.

"You're learning Icelandic?"

"Anglo-Saxon. I'm translating *Beowulf.*" She saw his eyes brighten. "The word *drottinn,* that's lord, isn't it? It's *dry-ten* in Anglo-Saxon."

"Good, good!" Svenn nodded. "And the sagas, have you read any of the sagas?"

"I plan to translate *Burnt Njal.*"

He nodded again. "The sagas are life," he said, and continued:

> *Neither gleams the gold in me,*
> *Nor gaudy letters shine.*
> *My beauty all I hold in me,*
> *For learning makes me fine.*

"Oh," she said, astonished. Uncle Svenn had just spoken more consecutive words to her than he had ever done in her lifetime. He was still talking.

"You want to learn more of your heritage," he said, "reading the old sagas and keeping the Viking spirit—undefeated, no matter what befalls, mastering your life." He lit a cigarette with a shaky hand.

"Amma doesn't like anyone to smoke in the house," said Catherine primly.

"She never minded me," he said and scowled.

> *O woe to those and woes to those*
> *My lineage betray.*

Kate remembers two pictures she had seen on one of her forages in the attic: two formal photographs, dated only a few months apart. The one taken in June 1914 showed Svenn in his graduation gown. The austere medieval robe complemented his clean-shaven Viking face with its firm lips and bright, hopeful eyes. The other picture, dated November 1914, probably posed for a Christmas-going-away gift, revealed Svenn in an army private's uniform. This time the eyes were steely and the lips were tight with determination. Had Catherine seen all that, or is Kate editorializing after the fact?

"You were in the war," Catherine said then over the funeral-baked *vínar terta*. "The First World War."

"The war to end all wars," he nodded.

She looked at Svenn's bleary eyes and remembered them steely. He looked away and shrugged with a tired lift of the shoulders and a crooked lift of his mouth.

"I survived," he said. "Not the same man they sent away, but I came back, and fell into a Drowning Pool."

"What's that?" asked Catherine, puzzled.

He paused and then recited again, "'There lies less good than most believe in ale for mortal men'—so goes the *Edda*."

"Snorri Sturluson was right!" said Catherine.

Svenn grinned at her, *grinned* at her, a gargoyle grin, grim and wry. "*Ja, ja,*" he said.

"And is it all come to this?" he asked. "To nothing?" And he recited again.

> *Of old there was nothing,*
> *Nor sand, nor sea, nor cool waves.*
> *No earth, no heaven above.*
> *Only the yawning chasm.*
> *The sun knew not her dwelling,*
> *Nor the moon his realm.*
> *The stars had not their places...*

He paused, trying to remember. "The stars had not their places," he repeated, and trailed off.

"What's that?" asked Catherine.

"The Norse story of creation," Svenn said impatiently. "Everyone knows Greek mythology. No one pays any attention to the Norse. You pay attention, Kate."

Kate remembers being surprised at his use of her adult name. People were just beginning to call her Kate. How did Svenn know that? He was just warming up.

"But then it began to take shape," he said.

"What did?"

"The universe. Pay attention, Kate. Yggdrasil, the ash-tree, sprang up to support the universe. Three roots there are to Yggdrasil. Hel lives beneath the first; beneath the second, the Frost Giants; and men beneath the third."

He paused while he lit a new cigarette from the smouldering butt, squinting against the smoke.

"Your Amma thought Canada was the land of the Frost Giants."

"Did she?"

He nodded.

"I suppose because it's so cold."

"No, because it's white and lonely and austere."

"Oh!" Kate remembered exclaiming, not because of whatever Svenn thought Amma saw in Canada, but because Svenn was talking so much. He wasn't finished.

"Above is Asgard, the home of the gods, and the bridge between Asgard and Midgard, where men dwell, is called Bifrost. It is a quivering rainbow, like me. See?" He put his cigarette in his mouth and held out both his hands to show her how they quivered.

"See, Kate?"

"Yes, quivering," she said. "I see."

The smoke curled up from his mouth, making his eyes water.

"I never wanted the rainbow," he said. "I wanted to find the Well of Knowledge."

"Me too. Maybe it runs in the family."

"A serpent gnaws at the roots of Yggdrasil and someday the whole world will come crashing down."

"I think I remember something about that—Ragnarok, isn't it?"

"Good, yes, Ragnarok—the final battle between the gods and the powers of evil."

"And the gods lose."

"They always lose. Like me. I always lose." He stubbed out his cigarette in his saucer stood up and said, "And the flames of the land will light the final darkness until they burn out and there is only blackness and defeat."

"Are you talking about the war?" asked Catherine.

He said the Icelandic swear word, the one she'd been told never to say, because it was about the Enemy, so her *amma* had told her. She watched her uncle leave the kitchen and then saw him going down the walk leading from the house. He hadn't bothered to pull on a coat or cap against the bitter cold. Catherine never saw him again.

Later that winter Svenn spent too long in a snow bank one night and died of pneumonia a week later.

Not a Viking hero at all, thinks Kate, rounding off memory. And yet—maybe he was. The whole idea was supposed to be endurance, wasn't it? Victory was irrelevant; everyone is defeated in the end. The important thing is to hang on, against impossible odds. Destroyed by the war, as surely as if he had been mowed down by cannon fire, Svenn had endured in his own way. He left Kate his Icelandic books.

Andscotinn!

—YOUR LOVING NIECE, BETTY JANE

CHAPTER TWELVE

LORE

—LETTER TO MY COUSIN'S GRANDDAUGHTER

DEAR HERBORG:

You won't remember this but the first time I visited Iceland, in the summer, when I was a guest of your great-grandmother, Halldóra, your grandmother Hebba and I took you to a Reykjavik park to play. It was fun. (I swear I saw an elf on the balance beam behind you.) I had my first glimmer of this book that day. I was reading troll stories and had found a children's book about a troll called Flumbra— lovely name! I didn't know whether children in Iceland believed in trolls. I wanted to reassure you—or myself? "Yes, Herborg, there is a Flumbra!" Your grandmother tells me you are ten years old now. Do you still believe in trolls? I hope so, because I want to discuss the ancient lore with you.

I know adults believe in trolls, also elves and fairies. I notice the word is the same in Icelandic for both elf and fairy—*álfur,* not to be confused with *Huldufolk*—Hid-Folk, or the hidden people, although they are sometimes called elves, too. Then there are changelings; sendings and emissaries; ghosts and ghouls and fetches. In my research into the lore and superstitions of Iceland and their transition to New Iceland, I have come upon several writers who believe that Thomas Edison was the biggest ghost buster of them all: electric light dispelled ghosts along with shadows. Our late Canadian media guru, Marshall McLuhan, said that electricity was instant information. I guess it's also instant debunking. I don't know, though, that I could live happily in a world entirely without shadows. Again, it must be race memory that makes me feel that way. Shadows conjure images, as the word implies, the very stuff of imagination. My friend W.H. Auden would agree with me. He believed in "as much neurosis as the child can bear," that is, in quirks and shadows and things that go bump in the night. The dark evokes too much magic to give it up, don't you agree? Darkness conjures up all kinds of images, seen best in the shimmering light of the mind's eye. Darkness, isolation and belief, but the most powerful of all is darkness. That's where trolls thrive, as you know. They turn to stone if they are caught in sunlight. Judging by all those rocks, I'd say that Iceland has more petrified trolls than anywhere else in the world. Therefore, by corollary, Iceland must have more trolls.

Icelanders' word for troll, I found, is *tröll*, not surprisingly, because it's their word, but the root is interesting. It derives from Old Norse, *troll* (cf. Danish *trold*, an elf), a giant, a demon. The verb *troll* means "to turn or revolve" (obs), from the Middle English, "to roll, to wander"; Old High German, "to run with short steps" (also to ramble, to stroll, whence comes *trollop*, a slattern, a loose woman, a prostitute). In Iceland, trolls are ogres, clumsy giants, usually malevolent, and, fortunately for us humans, not very smart. They are terrifying and vicious, but like other fantastic creatures in Iceland they have a sense of fair play and a strong sense of gratitude, that is, like elves, they're quick to acknowledge when they owe you one and swift in their repayment of a debt. I have come across several versions of a story that tells of a female troll's gratitude to a young man for a kindness to her children—he fed them—and her generous reward. Food is important to trolls, as it was to most hungry Icelanders in centuries past.

A significant Scandinavian influence on my writing is "The Three Billy Goats Gruff." Do you have the story in Icelandic, Herborg? Do you remember that the nemesis under the bridge, waiting to eat anyone who dared cross it, was a troll? It was my boys' favourite bedtime story for a while. Every night they looked forward to that delicious shiver when a goat tried to trip undetected over the bridge and the troll roared, "Now I'm coming to eat you up."

I wrote a puppet play based on the story and called it "The Bridge Over the River My," because the troll, Tronkite, insisted "It's my bridge." Like most trolls, he was a bit slow. One of my favourite scenes from my early writing occurs in this play, when the biggest, dumbest goat confronts Tronkite and they have an argument both have difficulty following. You should know, Herborg, I am not a violent person, so, although there is a battle, it is resolved short of bloodshed by the goats' resourceful goat herd, Peter, who suggests a peaceful solution.

"A troll bridge?" asks Tronkite, puzzled. He already has a troll bridge. No, a *toll* bridge.

If everyone pays to go across the bridge, the troll will have enough money to buy food so he won't have to eat the creatures who want to get to the other side. This was the cue for a collection of puppets to parade across the bridge, and for the production department of the puppetry troupe to go wild with their craft.

All I knew about trolls then I put into that play: they were green, slightly mildewed from living in damp places under bridges and waterfalls. This one had, according to the book I read nightly to my sons, "eyes as big as saucers and a nose as long as a poker," all the better to fight with and gobble up the goats. Oh, and they were Scandinavian.

I dwell on trolls as I will soon dwell on the *Huldufolk* because some of these creatures crossed the ocean with the Western Icelanders and, like them, have suffered a sea change. My search turned up 13 pages of web sites for trolls or troll appearances on the Internet, and most of them are North American, having little to do with Iceland. There seems to be a new, unspoken agreement about what trolls look like. Toy and gift shops sell troll dolls in various sizes (made of soft enough plastic to be, if not cuddly, at least compliant) with bug-eyes and multihued hair. Some are so tiny they fit on the end of pencils. They are cute, they are kitschy and they have nothing to do with frozen rocks and menacing lava castles. I begin to feel sorry for trolls.

The Western *Huldufolk* have undergone a similar fate; they have been trivialized beyond recognition, were any of them foolish enough to return to Iceland. Do you know the origin of the *Huldufolk*, Herborg? Back there in the beginning, after the apple fell from the tree, Adam and Eve had a passel of brats. One day God told Adam he was going to pay the family a visit. With so little warning, Eve didn't have time to clean up all the kids so she hid the dirty ones. When God came and met her presentable, washed children, he asked if these were all, and she assured him that they were. Well, of course, God knew everything. He said, and these must be his exact words, I have read them so often: "That which has been hidden from me shall be hidden from men."

Thus *Huldufolk*—hidden people—I was going to say made their appearance, but actually they made their disappearance in the world. They, too, are known as elves. They prefer to live in hills, mounds and caves, but some of them live closer to human dwellings and make do with a large rock at the bottom of the garden. Some of them get along very well with humans, to the extent that elfwomen will mate with human men, and less frequently, human women with elfmen. Apparently the males can be *unelfed*. The big problem is what to do about the child or children resulting from the union. (It's that age-old, thorny problem of bringing up the children Catholic.) A man seems to get the better deal if he takes up with an elfwoman, although he had better be good to her or she will leave him and he will go mad. As for the elfmen, they come in handy when someone has to be blamed for a surprise pregnancy, which used to happen to dairy maids left alone for the summer to look after a hilltop dairy. There is a distinctly sexual undertone in the elf stories.

Learning all this, I could understand that, in the beginning at least, Hid-Folk/elves were the same size as humans, and scarcely distinguishable, unless you knew what to look for: no ridge between the nostrils, and so on. Over the centuries, however, they began to shrink, so that they are now Little People. Still, they wield great power.

Whether or not they are neighbours or mates, *Huldufolk* seem to be a little like Mary Norton's Borrowers in their habits, except that they eventually return the things they borrow from humans, at least, according to some stories. This is one annoying habit they have carried into the New World. In his *Icelandic-Canadian Oral Narratives*,[1] Magnús Einarsson quotes a number of different accounts of borrowings by Hid-Folk. The items are kept for about a year before they show up again, exactly where they were last seen. These creatures sound very human.

In Iceland they were not only human-size but also handsome, and beautifully dressed, with rich clothes and jewels, again, according to humans who have seen them. It's up to the *Huldufolk* to decide whether they want to be seen or not, or even whether or not to be corporeal. Some stories tell of a human male lying with a beautiful *huldakona* (hidden woman) and being unable to feel her body in bed beside him. Like most of the supernatural beings in Iceland, Hid-Folk are capricious in their dealings with humans, being kind or nasty by turns. A lot depends on how they are treated.

---

1 Hull: Canadian Museum of Civilization, 1991.

The Icelandic elf people were wont to swap children with humans. If the elves had a sickly baby, they would substitute it for a human one, expecting that humans might give the elfin child the care it needed. If the humans suspected that the child was elfin, they would not always care for it, in fact, they might deliberately mistreat it or allow it to die. The story of the Changeling Child was a convenient myth people adopted as a way of acknowledging a damaged baby and justifying its neglect in order to dispose of it.

I have read half a dozen reports—not stories, but newspaper reports—of *Huldufolk* who have blocked major construction projects because a road or a building was going to be put up on the site of one of their dwelling places. When machinery breaks down and other accidents occur in Iceland, people know it's the *Huldufolk's* doing and that steps must be taken to placate them. So a detour around a rock is built into a straight road, or a building is relocated, or, according to one story, construction workers will carefully move a very large boulder, at great expense, instead of dynamiting it out of the way, because it's someone's home, some *Huldufolk's* home, that is.

It took a short while for the *Huldufolk* to turn up in Gimli, Manitoba. Apparently, none of them was willing to be part of the first exodus. When they did come, there were no rocks or hills with caves to live in, not on scrub prairie with a huge lake on one side, so they had to adapt to a new life style. Two brave little *Huldufolk* who made the move have been duly reported in the pages of Kathleen Arnason's book, *The Story of the Gimli Huldufolk.*[2] Writing in the first person of one of the two little men, named Snaebjorn and Snorri, Arnason tells us that they first moved into the second storey of the Tergesen store (built in 1898), so I guess that makes us sort of related. Later they moved into the Gimli Public School, which was built in 1915,

2 Gimli: Saga Publishing Company, Huldufolk House, 1993

according to the sign on the front of the building, and lived in the attic. The first sightings didn't come until the school was destined to be torn down. They appeared to an old man called Leo, whom they remembered as a tall, gangly kid when he was going to the school. I suppose in the same way that *Huldufolk* make their wants known in Iceland when a road or building is in their way, Snorri and Snaebjorn persuaded Leo[3] to save the school. He has been indeed the mover and shaker behind the restoration of the old building, which now houses the Gimli Heritage Museum. Mover, shaker, and builder, Leo was the one who carefully saved the maple floors, stripped and polished them and lovingly relaid them in the old classrooms, which now house, in addition to the museum, the Gimli Town Office, a small art gallery, and the headquarters of the Icelandic National League. He also built a new attic for the *Huldufolk.*

I almost missed it, because it was off season for tourists and for Huldufolk. Tucked in a corner on the second floor is a narrow, small-scale, beautifully made, winding staircase to an unfinished attic. I bumped my head going up, so I was more careful coming down. Up there, it's an attic, that's all, but Herborg, you would love it. There are two very small beds and two small chairs flanking a chess set, which looks as if it had just been abandoned when I came up. In the front corner there's a little bookcase, hinged so that it opens on a tiny, secret hidey-hole. The front window looks down on the flower beds, parking lot and giant-size chess set for people. If you raise your eyes, you can see Lake Winnipeg about three blocks away. This attic was Leo's idea.

Leo's wife, Jean, oversees the making of the Huldufolk dolls by the *Huldufolk* Moms. They are replicas of artist

---

3 His name is Dr. Leo Kristjanson, and he has his Ph.D. in economics and history (U. Wisconsin) and his LL.D. from the University of Winnipeg.

Jerry Johnson's idea of what the Gimli *Huldufolk* look like: enantiomorphs,[4] almost identical, but with their colours reversed. One wears a red hat and blue scarf, the other a blue hat and red scarf. The dolls can be purchased from the Icelandic National League or from Tergesen's Store. There is also available, in addition to *Huldufolk* T-shirts, a sequel to Kathleen Arnason's best-selling first book, called *The Huldufolk: Forever Friends*.[5]

This is where the real difference between the old world and the new is most apparent, in the *Huldufolk*, who have become dolls and the subject of two children's books; and in trolls, who have become cute ornaments and mascots. It's no one's fault. The least guilty are the Western Icelanders themselves. It's what has happened to tales, folklore, myths, legends, superstitions and magic in the 20th century. Fairy tales were originally told to adults; when the brothers Grimm set them down, they were illuminating a people's belief systems. As the shadows were dispelled and pagan superstitions lost their power, such beliefs were replaced by more commonplace, common sense views. The earlier tales controlled people's minds with their violence and malevolence; now the trolls and their cousins have retreated to the nursery. They have been bowdlerized, domesticated and in many cases animated and hoked up by Disney. I suppose there are so many horrific things in the world today that we need our tales and legends coated with sugar—or aspartame. A recent release by the Book-of-the-Month Club of *Grimm's Grimmest*[6] reveals how bloody, cruel and unforgiving the old stories really were. They were never intended for children. These days Stephen King makes up for the softening of old tales.

---

4 In Martin Gardner's book *The Annotated Alice* (New York: Clarkson N. Potter, Inc., 1960) he identifies Tweedledum and Tweedledee as what geometers call enantiomorphs, mirror-image forms of each other.

5 Also by Kathleen Arnason, illustrated by Jerry Johnson. Gimli: Saga Publishing Company, Huldufolk House, 1997.

6 San Francisco: Chronicle Books, 1997.

It's not hard to figure why the old ghost stories continued on this side of the ocean. Although it lacks rocks, mountains, glaciers and lava, Gimli at least could offer long, cold, lonely, dark nights with lots of threatening shadows and plenty of time for the imagination to mould them into ghosts and ghouls. There were references to ghouls in the Gimli Heritage Museum and the popularity of stories about them. Some people acquired a reputation for such tales. This made me wonder if the stories about ghouls may have been the reason for the nickname given to the first Western Icelanders. They were called "ghoulies." My mother hated the term. I only offer it here because it solves a mystery. Perhaps the epithet came from the ghouls who followed the settlers. Just a theory.

I can't maintain that Icelanders were unique in their superstitions and otherworldly beliefs. The Swiss psychologist Carl Jung suggested that there is a collective unconscious—that part of the mind that abides in every human being and every culture. It's true that over the centuries magical creatures have existed in every country in the world, differing very little from place to place, although the differences are significant. Ireland has its leprechauns; England its brownies; Finland its mermen and magicians; Denmark its nixies (water goblins); Sweden its house spirits; Norway its trolls—shared with Iceland. Iceland has no guardian house spirits, but it does have the *jola sveinar*— the Yule fellows—12 greedy, noisy trolls who appear one by one from the 12th of December right through to Christmas Day and then disappear one by one until they've had their fill of pot-scraping, spoon-licking, and so on. At Christmastime in Iceland the stores are full of cards and calendars as well as little dolls and ornaments, decorated with these not-so-jolly guys. These days they're running a losing battle with Santa Claus. The world is becoming too homogenous.

Ghosts are usually nastier than trolls. They're also godless.
I read an estimate, not to be taken lightly, that one out of
every 500 people you meet in Iceland is a ghost. For har-
rowing ghost stories, read some of the old Icelandic folk
tales.[7] One ghost story is of a night ride that a woman
called Guðrun takes with her lover who she doesn't know
is dead. He keeps trying to call her name, but he can't say
Guðrun because *Guð* means God, and, godless pagan that
he is, he cannot bring himself to name God. So he keeps
moaning "Garun, Garun." She does manage to escape,
dumping him in an open grave on the way by.

I don't like sendings and emissaries, supernatural mes-
sengers sent to get you. Lappish Breeches are gruesome; I
don't want to talk about them. Fetches, though, are fascinating, and they, too, have crossed the ocean, according to
Magnús Einarsson's informants.

A fetch *(fygja)* is a person's wraith or double—a ghost—
that usually goes ahead of the person it is attached to,
providing early warning signs of the person's arrival to
those with second sight *(skygn)*. The *Canadian Oxford
Dictionary* has it as: "a person's wraith, or double," and so
does the *Dictionary of Newfoundland English*: "an appari-
tion or double of a living person, the appearance of which
often portends death or disaster; ghost; also known as a
token, a vision or sign, if one sees an absent friend that
that person will die within a year." Fetches run in families, or I should say, second sight runs in families.

Icelandic folk tales were more leisurely in their style
than the other Scandinavian stories, perhaps because the
nights were (a little) longer. I think they exhibited the
love of detail and the lively sense of scene because of the
influence of the sagas. Generally there were four main
types. First, there are the "eye witness" accounts, using

---

7 Available in an inexpensive collection published by the Iceland Review Library,
first published in 1977 and which goes into printing after printing.

both ancient legends and lore and what we today call urban myths—events closely related to the lives of the narrators and their listeners. These are supposed to have been told to the narrator by his/her cousin's grandmother— that would be on the other side. Second, there are "if-wishes-were-horses" stories: tales of buried treasure, and dreams-come-true, some of them as simple as a good catch of fish every day (guaranteed, for example, by a troll's gift of a magic fish hook). The third type of story is the myth of creation, common to cultures everywhere (how the leopard got its spots; how the loon got its necklace). Finally, there is storytelling for the sheer fun of it, for entertainment value. Whether they're "gotcha!" tales, romances or humorous accounts of feckless householders or dumb trolls, they serve to pass the long hours of a sub-Arctic night. Gifted storytellers were worth their weight in herring.

They still are and they still have a faithful audience. Only the medium has changed. Magnús Einarsson and his old-timers worry that there will soon be no one left who remembers or tells the old stories, and they're probably right. Television and film have taken over from the human voice weaving a spell in the darkness of the *baðstofa*. But the tales remain the same, with one addition. Extraterrestrials have joined the party.

—FROM YOUR SECOND COUSIN TWICE REMOVED,
BETTY JANE

CHAPTER THIRTEEN

FOUR TALES
—LETTER TO MY YOUNGEST GRANDCHILDREN

DEAR EMILY AND DAVID:

I have written these tales for you, my youngest grand-children. Some of them are to grow on. I hope you like them.

A TROLL TALE

Once upon a time there was a little troll named Sigurf. He was not really little, about six feet and still growing, but he looked small when he stood beside the other trolls. He didn't mind because he didn't stand beside the other trolls very often, just his mother. He didn't mind her, either.

"Mind what I say," Mother Laraf would say. "You must-n't stay out after light. You'll catch your death. Look at what happened to Cousin Halldorf."

Sigurf knew what had happened to Cousin Halldorf. Everyone knew that. Cousin Halldorf stood outside the cave where Sigurf lived with his mother. Sigurf saw the big rock every evening when he went out to play and every morning when he came in for bed. Halldorf hadn't hidden from the sun in time. So there he was, a rock for ages.

"You be careful," said Sigurf's mother.

"Yes'm," said Sigurf and stood still while she kissed him before she pushed him out into the dark.

What Sigurf's mother didn't know because he didn't tell her was that Sigurf was afraid of the dark. Really scared. He saw moving shadows behind every rock. There were a lot of rocks out there, grim reminders of other night-trolls who hadn't made it home before the sun came up. Sigurf was sure the shadows were the restless remainders of the luckless ones and he was sure they would trip him if he came too close to them. But it was hard to stay away from rocks. Besides, he needed them. His mother said so.

She taught Sigurf to count the rocks. Seven rocks to the left was their neighbour's cave. Ten rocks out, then straight up, counting every other rock, that was the way to Sigurf's father's cave. Valgarf was the lookout for the troll tribe and lived on the mountaintop most of the year. Sigurf's mother visited him in the winter when the nights were long, and he used to ski down for the winter solstice. They didn't dare meet during the summer. It was so bright that all the night-trolls had to stay indoors. At its worst, in mid-summer, there was barely enough twilight to skulk in.

Third rock from the cave, that was Sigurf's favourite. Out past Cousin Halldorf the path dipped downward to a stream at the bottom of the valley. It was easy to run down but it was slower coming back up. That was how Halldorf was caught. The morning mist had cleared too fast. The sun was up before he knew it and there were no shadows.

"Shadows are your friends," Sigurf's mother had told him. "You can hide in a shadow."

But Sigurf was afraid of shadows. For one thing, the shadows made it hard for him to find his way. Sigurf had no sense of direction. His mother often said he couldn't find his way out of a one-way cave, but she didn't know how right she was. She didn't know he still couldn't find his way anywhere without counting rocks.

To count rocks you had to be able to see them. Sigurf had trouble seeing in the dark. That was the worst of it. Night-trolls are supposed to have excellent night vision. Sigurf might as well shut his eyes, for all he could see. He needed some light.

Moonlit nights weren't so bad, except for the scary shadows. By moonlight Sigurf could see well enough to count the rocks. But they made long shadows in the blue light and they frightened Sigurf. He loved the northern lights best. Bright moving sheets of colour swept across the night sky and gave the young troll enough light to see his way but not enough to cause shadows.

"When are the northern lights coming, Mama?" asked Sigurf.

"Not for a long time," said Laraf. "You ask me that every night, Sigurf. The lights are gone for a while. Haven't you noticed the nights are getting shorter? Now run along, and be sure you come home before light." She gave Sigurf a kiss, pushed his hair out of his eyes, and sighed as he shuffled out of the cave. She had a lot to do before dawn.

Sigurf stood outside the cave in the darkness and looked around, blinded by the darkness. Gradually his eyes became accustomed to the gloom. The sky was overcast and he could make out only a few cold, distant stars. Haldorf looked dark and foreboding. Sigurf shivered and looked up.

"Star light, star bright," he said. "Stay out and play tonight."

One star winked at him. That gave Sigurf courage so he started down the path to the stream, not daring to look too long at the rocks that marked his way.

Once at the stream, Sigurf forgot his fears for a while. This was his favourite spot, where the water formed a smooth pool before rushing on down the valley. He picked up pebbles and skittered them across the surface one at a time. He'd been practising. He could make a flat stone skip three times. He picked up a neat, flat one and leaned sideways so he could throw it parallel to the water. Just as he was about to let it fly, he heard a sound. The stone left his hand and fell to the ground.

What was that noise? Sigurf cocked his head and listened. There it was again, a soft mewing that came from a rock behind him. A mewing rock? Sigurf stared at it.

"Who's there?" he asked. He didn't go any closer.

The noise stopped, but there was no answer. Sigurf ventured a step closer to the rock.

"Is anyone there?" he asked more loudly.

He heard a whimper, cut off as if a hand had clapped over a telltale mouth. Whatever it was, it sounded more scared than Sigurf. He moved closer still.

"I won't hurt you," he said. "I'm scared too."

The rock was silent, as if it was listening.

"Really?" the rock said.

"Really," said Sigurf, and waited. He squinted at the rock. It was so hard to see in the dark.

Out from behind the rock stepped the palest creature Sigurf had ever seen. Her hair was long and white, her face was white and her long dress was white. Standing now in front of the black rock she had been hiding behind, she seemed to glow in the dark. Sigurf could see her very well.

"I can see you!" he said.

"You said you wouldn't hurt me," she said.

"Would you like me to show you how to skip stones on the water?" Sigurf asked.

Sigurf had never thrown stones better. With his pale friend shimmering beside him, he could see what he was doing. The two of them played for hours. When they tired of throwing stones they sat down beside the stream and built a cairn.

For this they needed larger rocks but there were plenty around. Sigurf was able to pick the best ones because he could see. The cairn was almost as high as Sigurf could reach. As he put the last rock on top it glinted in the light.

The light! The sun was coming up. In fact, it was up, behind the mountain. Sigurf knew that his father would already have seen it and ended his night chores, safe in his cave for the day. Now the sun was peeking between the craggy peaks and darting bright gleams down into the valley. Sigurf had to get home. He had no time to lose.

"Gotta go now," he said to his new friend, and ran.

He made his way up the path as quickly as he could, dodging the light as he went. He jumped behind a rock, peering out until a shadow made it possible for him to run to the next one.

His chest hurt by the time he saw Cousin Halldorf looming in front of the cave. He'd never been so glad to see that big rock. He flew to it and put his arms around it, panting heavily.

Sigurf's mother ran out of the cave carrying a huge umbrella. Under its shade she hurried to Sigurf, grabbed him by the ear and pulled him in close to her.

"Stay close to me," she said. Looking like a very large mushroom with four legs, they scurried to the shelter of the cave.

Not a moment too soon. The sun was well above the mountaintop, shining down on everything, clear and bright and merciless.

"It's going to be a terrible day," said Laraf, "absolutely cloudless. You should have known that when you saw the stars come out. What were you doing?"

"Building a cairn," said Sigurf.

"Oh!" Laraf was surprised. Sigurf had never built a cairn before. She suspected it was because he couldn't see well enough to find the right rocks for it. It must have been a very clear night.

She didn't have the heart to scold him. He knew as well as she did how close he had come to being a rock like Cousin Halldorf. He looked tired. She looked at him again. He also looked happy. Most of the time her son looked sad, or more often, bewildered. This morning he looked happy.

"Sleep well," was all Laraf said as she tucked Sigurf into his moss bed for the day.

Sigurf played with his new friend every night. They were so busy and found so many games to play that he never seemed to find time to talk, to ask her where she came from or who she was. One night he remembered to ask her name.

"Hebbaf," she said. "Come on, let's play pie."

She showed him how to make a pie circle with rocks and then to make slices inside the circle with more rocks and then how to jump from slice to slice in a game of tag. Then she declared he was ready for hopscotch. Sigurf had never heard of it.

"There are perfect pebbles for hopscotch downstream a bit," she said. "And a flat place where we can draw the map, and sharp stones to draw it with."

"How far downstream?" Sigurf asked anxiously.

"Not far."

It was, though, farther than Sigurf had ever gone. And it took a long time to make the hopscotch map. Hebbaf was very particular, choosing the flattest place for it, so that took time. Then it took time to find sharp stones to cut the lines. Then it took even longer to find a perfect flat pebble for each of them to throw. She was just starting to show Sigurf how the game worked when the sun came up.

The nights had been getting shorter but Sigurf hadn't noticed. He had been so happy and busy with his new friend that the time had flown by. Now he looked up in horror as clear, bright sunshine began to flood the valley.

"I don't have time to get home," he said. "I'm going to end up like Cousin Halldorf."

"Come with me," said Hebbaf and ran in the opposite direction from Sigurf's home.

"Where?" shouted Sigurf.

"My cave," she said. "You'll be safe there." So Sigurf ran after her.

They ran in the shadow of a mountain that curved close to the stream. This deep shadow, falling across the hop-scotch map, was the reason Sigurf hadn't noticed the light fanning across the top of the mountain. Hebbaf was splashing into the stream ahead of him. He caught up with her as she lifted her dress so as not to get the hem wet.

"We'll take the shortcut," she said, and turned to wade deeper into the water.

"Stop!" said Sigurf. He was afraid of drowning, too—not drowning exactly. His mother had told him about night-trolls caught swimming in the ocean when the sun rose. They had become the reefs and rocks sailors cursed when they ran their boats into them. Sigurf didn't want to be a rock in the stream. He hated getting his feet wet.

His feet were wet now. He shivered as the cold water ran over them, shivered, but was rigid with fear. He was going to be a rock!

"Come on!" shouted Hebbaf and pulled him farther into the water.

It was shallow. A shoal ran down the middle of the stream. From there it was an easy crossing on stepping stones that looked almost as if they'd been put there on purpose.

"This is my bridge," said Hebbaf as she jumped from stone to stone just ahead of Sigurf. Then she disappeared.

One instant she was there, the next instant she was gone. Sigurf looked at the grey wall of the mountain looming up above him and the sun above that was about to blaze down and burn him stiff.

Suddenly a hand reached out of a scraggly bush in front of him and pulled him in. Sigurf fell down, into the welcoming darkness of a small cave, right beside Hebbaf, who was still holding his hand.

"Are you all right?" she asked.

Sigurf nodded. "Wet, is all," he said. "How'd you know about this?

"I found it the night before I met you."

"Is this where you live?"

"I do now," Hebba smiled sadly. "Remember I was crying the night I met you?"

Sigurf remembered the mewing noise. That was crying?

"I was playing by the stream up the valley when I fell in and couldn't get out. It washed me all the way down to that bridge." She nodded at the stepping stones they had just crossed. "And then I just sort of fell into the bush, and this cave."

Sigurf looked around. It wasn't much of a cave, barely room for the two of them. He couldn't stand up straight without bumping his head. But it was dark and dry. They could stay here till nightfall. He looked at Hebbaf in bewilderment.

"You mean to tell me you've been staying here for a week and never told me?"

Hebbaf nodded.

"Why?"

"Promise you won't laugh at me," she said.

"I promise," said Sigurf.

"I'm afraid of the dark."

Sigurf laughed.

"You promised you wouldn't laugh!"

"I'm afraid of the dark, too," he said, and laughed again. "I thought I was the only one."

Then Hebbaf laughed with him.

Sigurf told her he would take her home to his mother and that Mother Laraf would solve everything. Hebbaf shared some berries and a bit of watercress with Sigurf and then the two tired young trolls slept until dark.

No need to worry now, thought Sigurf as he drifted off. After all, tomorrow is another night.

THE CHANGELING CHILD

Herborg had three other children and there was nothing wrong with them. Leif was thin and could run like the wind. Thordis was round and gentle and took care of creatures. Little Hebba smiled all the time. Now here was Baby Valgeir and he was nothing like the others. He was bony and cried all the time.

He seemed all right when he was born. "A fine, healthy boy," Aunt Lillja said after she looked him over. She wrapped him up and put the little bundle into Herborg's arms and he had nestled like a little bird, just like the others. But later in the night, when he was tucked in his cradle, dark clouds scudded across the sky and dimmed the moon and the baby cried out, a strange, harsh cry.

The fire had gone out, briefly. It dimmed, like the moon, Herborg thought. There was a flash of light—a bright spark, Herborg thought, a cinder leaping from the fire— and then darkness. She thought she heard a scuffle in the dark but it was probably one of the children turning in the bed the three of them shared. When one turned everyone turned, so Herborg could hear the rustling. Silence for a moment, then the fire flared up again and Baby Valgeir gave that strange, harsh cry. Herborg rose and went to him. He was uncovered and lay on his back with his arms thrown up, startled, stretching for something, as if someone had thrown him there in a hurry. He looked hungry.

From then on, he was always hungry. Herborg fed him 12 times a day and still he cried. He would start to nurse and then pull back gasping, clutching with his tiny hands, as if demanding more even as he fed. In between he was restless and angry. The other children tried to comfort him but he scowled and cried harder whenever they tried.

Leif played peekaboo, but Valgeir scowled and cried. Thordis stroked the baby's forehead and sang a lullaby, but Valgeir scowled and cried. Little Hebba clapped her hands and smiled, but Valgeir scowled and cried.

"I have never seen such a scowl on a baby," Herborg told Aunt Lillja when she came to call on them to see how mother and baby were doing. Aunt Lillja was Herborg's godmother, and midwife to half the countryside. Everyone called her Aunt Lillja. She was very old and very wise.

"In fact," said Herborg, "I have never seen such a scowl on anyone."

Lillja nodded gravely and peered over to look in Baby Valgeir's face. The only reason he was quiet was that Herborg was feeding him, and even then, not so quiet. As usual, he was ravenous. He slurped and sucked noisily, pulling back to gasp and scowl, then attacking again. Even when he was feeding he looked angry and hungry. He turned his eyes to Lillja for a moment and then looked away, back to his sucking, frowning a little. Lillja frowned, too.

"That is not," she said, "the baby I delivered."

Herborg looked sharply at Lillja's face. Aunt Lillja did not make wild announcements like that without reason. Herborg nodded, looking from Lillja's face to the baby's. Somehow, she was not surprised.

"It happened," she said, "the night the fire sputtered out, the night he was born."

"I think so," said Lillja. "Someone changed babies. Herborg," she said sadly, "you have a changeling child."

"No!" She cried out and clutched the baby, who struggled to be free of her tight embrace. But she knew it was true. "What can I do?"

"You have to make them take him back," said Lillja. "Take him back and bring you your own child. Your baby belongs in his own cradle."

"Why would they do this?" asked Herborg. She didn't have to ask who They were. No one had to ask.

"They have a sickly child and They don't know what to do with him. They're hoping that you can make him better."

"What's happening to my little Valgeir?"

For answer, Lillja shook her head. Herborg held the baby out from her body to look at him, at his poor, funny little screwed-up face. He looked back at her, pulling a jagged breath in his tiny racked frame. Did he seem relieved that she knew, or was that her imagination? She rose and put him in his cradle.

"What should I do?" she asked Lillja.

"I don't know whether you have the courage to do it," Lillja said cautiously.

"I want my baby back or not at all," said Herborg.

So Lillja told her what to do. And it was hard.

The next time the baby cried, Herborg didn't feed him. She couldn't bear to call him Valgeir anymore. She didn't know the name of this little stranger so she just called him the Baby. Sometimes she called him the Imp. No one noticed. The children were busy with their chores and games. Even little Hebba couldn't be bothered to spend much time with him anymore. So no one really noticed that she wasn't feeding him as often.

Instead, she was holding him over the fire, dangerously close, closer and closer.

"Smoke him out." That was what Lillja had said. "Threaten him. Make Them come for him before it's too late."

So Herborg held the infant over the hearth where the fire burned and the kettle boiled. So often she had warned the children to stay away, stay far away for fear of being burned or scalded. Now here she was, good mother that she was, holding a baby over the smoke and steam, inviting disaster. She held him at arm's length, taking care not to burn herself or get too hot, waving him back and forth, back and forth, while the heat swirled around him. He smiled!

The Baby drew a breath, and smiled! He really was an Imp from Hel!

But when Herborg put him back in his cradle, he slept.

She still fed him. She wasn't going to starve anyone to death. All she wanted to do was scare him, and scare his Folk, into giving back her son. So she fed him. But she also held him over the fire two or three times a day, threatening him with the fire, dangling him over the kettle, threatening him with the scalding, steaming contents. He loved it. He simply seemed to love it. He gurgled and smiled and took big breaths as the steam swirled up around his face. He must be trying to fool her, pretending to like it to make her stop doing it. She would not stop.

He behaved better. He took his feedings well, he slept well. He even smiled at the children when they stopped to look at him. Once, when Hebba played peekaboo, he even laughed!

Maybe They didn't understand. Maybe They thought if They held out, Herborg would forget this torment and teasing and go on as she had been, feeding and caring for a changeling child. The Imp himself seemed to have such a notion, behaving so much better, settling down so much more quickly. It had to end soon, this battle of wills. He was getting heavier all the time. Herborg was afraid she was going to drop him in the kettle. One night, finally, something happened. Or something didn't happen. The little one didn't wake up.

Herborg woke first in the morning after the first full night's sleep since the baby had been born. She opened her eyes to a quiet room. The other children were still asleep in the corner. Olaf was long gone, out to the nets. The fire was dying. It must be late morning. Herborg stretched and sighed and smiled. Such a good sleep! Suddenly she was wide awake. The Baby!

She jumped out of bed and ran to the cradle. The Imp was still asleep, breathing softly and peacefully, looking, Herborg had to admit, more like a sweet rosy baby than an Imp from Hel.

Later on that day of wonder, Aunt Lillja came to call.

"Is it working?" she asked as she came in. "Are They going to take him away and give you back your little Valgeir?" She didn't wait for an answer as she went to the Baby to see how he looked.

"I don't know," Herborg began, "but—" She was cut off by Lillja's shout from across the room.

"You did it!" she exclaimed. "The Imp is gone! You did it!"

Herborg, startled, looked sharply at Lillja and then at the baby. Lillja was right. The Imp was gone. He must have left in the night. They must have put a spell on the house so that They could come in and steal back their child and give Herborg hers. For here in Lillja's arms was her own sweet, dear, rosy little Valgeir, cooing and smiling happily. She reached out for him, to cuddle and feed.

"Don't stop doing what you were doing," warned Lillja. "Not right away. If They think you've tricked them, They might try to bring their own little one back."

"You are a wise woman, Lillja," said Herborg.

THE ELFWIFE

The first time Petur saw her, he was dazzled. He had pulled in his nets and he was spreading them over his boat to dry. He looked up to check the wind and he saw her coming down the shore towards him. She stepped lightly over the rocks, her soft sheepskin shoes scarcely seeming to touch the ground. She was quite small, very slim, a good head shorter than he was, but he couldn't seem to look away. She simply glowed. Her hair was paler than sunshine, her eyes as green as the sea on a summer afternoon. She stopped at the bow of his little boat and smiled at him.

He thought she had a wreath of seaweed in her hair but as she drew closer he saw it was a fine chain of gleaming green stones. Another, longer one was looped around her neck and hung between her breasts, held down by a bigger stone almost the size of Petur's fist. Her dress was a paler colour than the green stones, more like seafoam than cloth, he thought. It was very fine cloth, perhaps like silk. Petur had never seen silk. His eyes went back to the stone.

"Isn't that heavy?" he asked without thinking. She smiled and shook her head.

"Feel it and see," she said, lifting it up and offering it to him to heft the weight.

To do that he had to step closer to her. He stretched out a hand to hold the green stone she held out—not very far because it was attached to the chain of stones that hung around her neck. He stepped closer still and closed his hand around the stone, warm from her body. His hand brushed hers as he took it and he felt a spark shoot up his arm and through to his heart and loins. He had never felt a spark from the fire, but he thought it would be like that if it landed on his skin. He looked into the woman's eyes, and saw sparks in the depths, and it was all over for him.

"Come home with me," he said.

"Of course," she said. "That's why I came."

She took his hand and they walked back up the coast to the rocky path that led to Petur's shelter, part cave, part hut. She seemed to know where she was going. While they walked, Petur asked questions. She was vague in her answers. He couldn't make sense of most of them, but he found out all he needed to know for a while.

"My name is Eydis," she told him. "I live on the other side of the fjord."

"No one lives there," Petur said.

"I do," she said. "Did. Not anymore."

"Where, then?"

"With you now," she said, and smiled again. This time he smiled back.

"I knew that," he said, and kissed her.

After that, Petur's luck changed. His nets were always full. He had more than enough fish for himself and Eydis to eat and also to sell. Now that he had it, he never missed a day taking food to Guðrun, his mother, who lived in the small village farther inland. But he stopped going to church.

"Why don't you come to church anymore?" Guðrun asked one day when he brought her an especially nice fish.

"Eydis doesn't like it," he said. "She says it makes her head hurt."

"Too bad," said his mother.

"I'm sure she'll change her mind when the baby comes," Petur said.

That was how he told his mother the news. She didn't seem as happy as he thought she'd be, but then, his mother knew how much could happen to babies. Petur was the only grown son she had.

The baby's eyes were green, like her mother's, and her hair was as soft and pale as a duck's, the fine down that Petur collected from the nests and hidey-holes to fill a comforter for the little one.

"She needs a name," he said to Eydis.

"She has a name. I told you, her name is Sessclyja." It sounded like the soft sighing of water lapping on a sheltered shoal. Eydis smiled more at the baby now than she did at Petur. He supposed that was natural.

"She needs to be baptized," he said. "She needs to be given her name in church."

"No." Eydis frowned.

"Not yet," he reassured her. "When you are stronger."

"When is the baby going to be baptized?" asked Guðrun.

"Soon," he said.

"I will tell the priest."

One Sunday when Eydis was still asleep, Petur wrapped the baby in her down comforter and stole softly out of the hut with her. She didn't cry. She seldom cried. She fell asleep with the gentle rocking as Petur made his way up the hill to the church. His mother was waiting for him.

"Where's Eydis?" she asked.

"Asleep," he said. "She's not feeling well."

Guðrun held out her arms for the baby, who gave one short sharp cry as Petur handed her over.

Together, mother and son went into the church with the baby. People were waiting. The priest stood below the cross at the head of the church and smiled as they approached. The baby gave another small cry. The priest began to speak. He had to raise his voice as the wind outside rose to a whistling shriek.

The people stood when the priest ordered them to stand for the child and promise to care for her in their midst. Guðrun put the baby in the priest's arms as he prepared to anoint her head with holy water and pronounce her name. She was to be christened Guðrun after her grandmother: God's one.

A sudden gust of wind blew the church door open. Someone screamed on the same note as the wind and someone else ran to shut the door, too late. Eydis shut the door behind her and strode quickly down the aisle. She looked like a glowing sword.

"Not Garun," she said clearly. Her voice was soft but it seemed to ring out over the hushed heads of the people. "Not Garun."

She held out her arms for the baby and the priest wordlessly handed over the child to her. The baby gave a little sigh and nestled in her mother's arms, warm in her down comforter. Eydis turned to Petur.

"I trusted you," she said. "Weren't you happy?"

"I was," he said. "Happier than I have ever been."

"Or will ever be," she said, and turned and left him, walking out of the church slowly but steadily. No one stopped her.

Two things happened at once then. The church door banged behind her and Petur fell to the ground, mad.

He never spoke again.

No one ever saw the elf wife again, or her daughter, the baby Sesselyja.

Finally, here is a story based in the New World:

SECOND SIGHT: A GIMLI TALE

This happened to my cousin Loa when we were young. She was a year older than me so she was about nine when this happened, and I know it did because I talked to her right after it happened.

She was sleeping over with me at the cottage and she had to go to the bathroom in the night. She had a real house with an indoor toilet because she lived in Gimli all the time and went to school and everything, but I was only there in the summer so our cottage didn't have a bathroom. There was an outhouse behind some trees at the end of a path away from the house. Mom put a basin of soapy water on the back porch so we could wash our hands. I washed my hair in rainwater from the rain barrel, mostly cold, but Mom heated one kettle full if it was too cold. I guess we washed in the lake because I don't ever remember having a real bath all summer. When I was little, Mom gave me what she called a sponge bath and showed me how to have a full bath in a teacup of water, was how she put it. Every September, before I went back to school my father would take rubbing alcohol and cotton from his doctor's bag and wash off all the pine gum that had stuck to my arms and legs after climbing trees all summer. If the gum clots were too bad in my hair he took his surgical scissors to cut them out, so then I had spiky hair for a couple of months.

Loa's hair was white, well, I mean she wasn't old or anything, she was blond and so pale her hair looked white. I could see her in the dark, with her head glowing like a candle and I could have seen her that night if I'd been awake. Didn't do her any good, though, because she was inside her head and couldn't see by the light of her hair. It was pretty dark out, too, just about a quarter of a moon, so that's why she kept the door open when she went to the outhouse, because it was really dark in there with no windows, just moon-shaped slits high up in the side walls.

So she was sitting there alone in the dark and trying to be quick when she saw me coming down the path, at least she thought it was me. At first she called out, softly, she said, so as not to wake my mother and brother in the cottage.

"Hi," she said. "Am I glad to see you. I never have to go to the bathroom at night, must have been all that lemonade we drank, and I forgot to go at bedtime because of that silly game."

Then she stopped talking because she noticed two things. One was that I—that is, if it was me—I wasn't saying anything. Two was that I wasn't moving. I was just standing there. Oh, and also I was taller than I usually was. That's when Loa finally realized it wasn't me. Well, if it wasn't me, who was it?

"Who is it?" she whispered then, whispered because all of a sudden her voice wasn't working too well. "Stop," she whispered as firmly as she could.

But it had already stopped. It just stood there, barring her path back to the house. By this time Loa was off the seat and ready to go back to bed and bury her head under the covers, even though it was hot, and kick me awake at the same time. But now this person, whoever it was, was barring her way, not saying anything though, just standing there with a tiny little beam of moonlight falling on its pale hair. Somehow it looked familiar.

Loa stood in the doorway of the outhouse—no way was she leaving it until the thing went away—and managed to squeak out a slightly louder voice.

"It's your turn now. You just go right in and I won't bother you a bit. I'm going back to bed."

But the thing didn't move and didn't speak.

"Pretty soon I'm going to have to scream," said Loa.

So then it started to sing. Sing! Can you imagine? Standing in the middle of the outhouse path in the middle of the night, it starts to sing. Not only that, Loa knew the song and all the words to it because her favourite aunt who was so sick had taught it to her. I don't remember what it was. She wasn't my aunt.

"Aunt Ruby, is that you?" said Loa, forgetting for a minute that her aunt was sick and couldn't walk, let alone sing. "Boy, am I glad to see you! You shouldn't go wandering around in the dark scaring people like that—" And then she stopped, because suddenly she remembered that her aunt was very sick.

"What are you doing here?" she asked, only she said it was more like a shriek. "You'll catch your death—I mean—it can't be good for you to be out of bed and walking around at night."

Her aunt, if it was her aunt, just smiled and twirled around as if she was dancing, the way she used to do before she got so sick that her bones started to melt.

"That's a stupid question," Loa answered herself. "You're dancing, of course. It must be nice to be able to dance again, eh?"

Her aunt, if it was her aunt, just kept on twirling, a little faster.

"Well," said Loa very matter-of-factly, trying to be calm, "if it's all the same to you, Aunt Ruby, I'd like to go back to bed now, and I think you should do the same thing. I think you've had enough dancing for one night, don't you?"

Her aunt stopped dancing and stood very still and looked at Loa. She smiled a soft little smile and then she faded away, just faded away.

Loa stood there at the outhouse door and watched the path fade to darkness. A cloud slid across the sliver of moon and it was very dark. She didn't run back to the house, much as she wanted to, because she couldn't see. But she went as quickly as she could, being careful not to catch her bare toes in any twigs on the path. Her feet were cold by the time she crawled into bed beside me and she woke me up by putting them on my back. She did it on purpose.

As soon as I was awake, she told me everything she had seen, about her Aunt Ruby singing her favourite song and dancing in the skimpy moonlight. I remember listening sleepily and telling her to go back to sleep, which is what we both did.

The next morning, of course, wouldn't you know, when Loa went home she found out that her Aunt Ruby had died in the night. With a smile on her face.

I used to go and have coffee under the table at my *amma*'s house when I wanted something. Well, I didn't drink coffee, of course, but when I wanted a piece of *vínar terta* I'd go over at coffee time and she usually gave me two slices. But I wasn't supposed to be there because Amma and Mom and my aunts (Mom's two sisters) liked to gossip, so I sat under the table and Amma let me stay there and I listened to them all talking. I wanted to hear about Loa's Aunt Ruby. Loa's mother, Didda, was my mother's sister, which is how come Loa was my cousin, but Loa's Aunt Ruby was her father's sister which is how come she wasn't my aunt, too.

"Just passed away in her sleep," Aunt Didda was saying. "With a smile on her face." They were all silent, sipping coffee, and I guess they were nodding the way people do when they hear something sad and don't know what to say. Also, they knew this already. They were waiting for the rest. Me too.

"Loa saw her."

I knew that, but they didn't. I heard the cups being put down on the saucers while everyone, that is, Amma, my mother and Auntie Mug all leaned forward to listen harder. I heard the chairs creak.

"Loa does that."

Does she? I didn't know that. What does Loa do? I wondered.

"What does she do?" asked my mother.

"Oh, Bibba, you know. I've told you before when she does something like this. Never quite like this before, though."

"I guess I never listened hard enough. I didn't want to scare Heather." Wouldn't you know with all those lovely Icelandic names and nicknames to choose from, my mother would give me a plain name like Heather?

"She and Loa are such good friends, I didn't want to spoil it by talking about Loa's *skygn*."

Skygn? What was Mom talking about? I almost asked out loud but I knew she'd shoo me out. I bet even Amma was feeling funny about me being there, but she never ratted on me.

Amma was talking, very matter-of-factly, probably trying to soothe me as well as her daughters. "Lots of children have second sight. They lose it as they get older," she said.

"Loa's not losing hers, it's getting stronger," said Aunt Didda. "At first, when she was little, you remember, I thought it was cute when she seemed to know what I was thinking. I'd be planning to invite someone over for coffee and she'd ask me when is soanso coming and that's who I was thinking of. And there was that night when Walter came home late from work, even later because he stopped to watch the fire truck at a fire and Loa woke up wanting a drink of water and started chattering about the fire. I thought she'd been having a bad dream but when Walter came home and told me about it—you remember, when the Kristjansons' house burned down? It was the same time he was watching that Loa saw it."

My aunts and Amma didn't seem to think much of all that but I thought it was creepy. They all said oh sure, kids did that, and talked about other kids that did that. I never did that, so Mom had nothing to say. She just repeated what Amma said, that kids grow out of it.

"Not Loa," said Aunt Didda firmly. "Last spring she knew that the cat was going to die, too. Remember, Furri was hit by a car last spring? Well, the night before, Loa was hugging it and crying, and I said why are you crying like that, there's nothing wrong with the cat. and she said Furri's going to die. We're all going to die, I said, so's the cat. No, she said, she's going to die tomorrow, so I have to hug her goodbye."

"Poor lamb," said Amma.

"The cat or Loa?" asked Mug, ready to laugh it off. Aunt Mug was always ready to laugh.

But no one laughed.

Me neither.

Well, this happened years ago. By the time I got to high school, I didn't see Loa much because I had a job in the city in the summer and stayed home. I heard when she got married. I was still in school. But I saw her after I got engaged and took Eric to meet the Gimli side of the family. Met her on the street, just like that. We laughed and hugged each other.

"I knew I was going to see you," Loa said. "I thought of you last night and I knew I was going to see you."

Oh, oh. Right away I thought of that strange conversation I had heard while I was under Amma's table. I didn't want to hear any more, but Loa was still talking. At least, she was happy. She didn't look worried so I guess it was all right. I introduced her to Eric and she shook his hand. Then she frowned.

"Don't trip," she said to him.

"What does that mean?" he asked.

"It doesn't mean anything," I said. "It's like a good-luck thing when people are getting married. Like when actors say 'break a leg'."

"That's it," said Loa.

And wouldn't you know, the next day, back in the city, when we were carrying stuff in from the car, Eric had so much in his arms he couldn't see in front of his feet and tripped on the steps and fell down and broke his leg. He married me in a cast.

I'm writing this down now because I saw Loa again, just hours ago. I brought the baby down for the family to see and Loa came with Aunt Didda and the others. Everyone oohed and aahed and said what a beautiful baby Sharon is, but Loa's eyes widened when she looked at her. I was watching Loa so I saw it. I saw her eyes widen and it wasn't with admiration. I'm sure it was fear. I'm sure she saw something. I was afraid to ask, but I had to know.

"What do you think?" I asked.

"I think she's lovely," said Loa.

"And?"

"Take good care of her."

"I will."

How could I ask her if something horrible was going to happen to my baby? I couldn't. I was afraid to. But Loa knew I needed to know more.

"Give her everything she needs to be strong," she said. "A child alone needs to be strong."

So it was Sharon she was afraid for, but not for the reason I thought. I wonder how it will happen to Eric and me?

—LOVE, AMMA

CANTO THREE
—LETTER TO W.H. AUDEN

I'm here in Gimli at the new museum
Checking out the precious artifacts.
But myths are pesky in that now you see'em
Now you don't. We all know life exacts
Penalties for dreams. I seek the facts:
When our settlers met reality
High hopes were dashed by actuality.

Perhaps the love of menacing landscape,
As with the food the taste for which seems strange,
Enabled them to hope and also scrape
A living from the bitter land. To change
Their skies might seem a fair exchange.
But why, in God's name, for a place like this?
Gimli is not the home of perfect bliss.

It must have been with wonder that they came,
Arriving at a new place with more ice
But also trees, more than they knew to name.
No wonder they called Gimli paradise.
At first they must have thought it worth the price,
But shortly after landing in the boondocks
The whole community came down with smallpox.

Ironic after trekking all that way,
At last arriving sound and safe from harm,

To be so needy and in such dismay
As to be forced to send out an alarm
Asking for a quick shot in the arm.
Their pride was hurt but no one was to blame
And they were mildly grateful all the same.

However, they survived and lived to thrive,
Adjusting well to their adopted country
Though they found it tough to stay alive.
Nothing prepared them for the shock of entry:
Manitoba weather was so wintry.
Would they have come this far if they'd been told?
Did the bright sunshine offset bitter cold?

You couldn't blame them if you'd heard them bleating.
Frostbite's not a pleasant thing, you know.
Even when there's modern central heating
It takes a hardy soul to love the snow.
The cold is still the reason people go;
You may have heard it said, a true report:
Manitobans are their chief export.

You think you had it tough when camping out
Among the rocks and lava on your trip,
But in your dream you'd never be as worn-out
As the folk who came here on a ship.
They must have wondered if they'd lose their grip.
You have to wonder at their desperation;
They really had no choice, nigh on starvation.

The world has changed so much since their first days
It might drive those folk mad to see it now.
I'm not so sure we'd win a lot of praise;
When new ways push the old aside, somehow
Bigger is not better, I'll allow.

Sometimes we lose the point and go astray.
Our heritage is tarnished with cliché.

If they came back to Gimli for a day
The settlers wouldn't recognize the town.
Their history gives the place a strange cachet
Appealing to the tourist coming down
To play, explore and eat. I see you frown.
You didn't like the food when you were there.
It takes a little time to enjoy skyr.

No matter, there are other things to do
In Gimli on the Celebration Day:
Parades and speeches, fun and ballyhoo.
I like the water sport for the blasé:
You charge a foe like a Don Quixote,
But on a plank. Be sure you are pre-shrunk
Before you try an Islendingadunk.

—BJW

CHAPTER FOURTEEN

IDENTITY AND SURVIVAL
—LETTER TO MY COUSIN

DEAR TERRY:

I'm addressing my last letter to you because you and I, although the same generation of Western Icelanders, have had quite different experiences. You're the family archivist; I'm the storyteller. I hope I got it right. If I didn't, it won't be for lack of trying or for lack of great support from you and Lorna.

Well, dear, as you've read these letters about my/our Icelandic heritage, you're probably wondering whether I even am Canadian. Let me tell you how Canadian I am. Growing up in Winnipeg, as you know, with childhood excursions to Gimli every summer, I felt as if I was at the exact centre of North America, of Canada, and that I had my fingers on the true heart of the Canadian experience. Sure, we all feel at the centre of our universe, dealing with experience from a self-centred consciousness. How could it be otherwise? But you have to admit I have an argument, geographically speaking. I remember when I made friends with the late theatre creator, John Hirsch, in the stacks at the University of Manitoba, he told me how he had come to choose Winnipeg as his home. Someone at the Jewish relief organization that was taking care of its European orphans after the Second World War showed John a map of Canada and asked him where he would like to live. He jabbed a finger at what looked to him to be the dead centre of the continent, as far away from any ocean as could be and presumably, therefore, safe. It was Winnipeg, he said. I remember nodding in total agreement. Not only safe, I thought, but balanced, free of the biased enthusiasms of people on either coast or in the busy urban centres of Ontario. Stuck in the middle, I felt I was a quintessential Canadian, able to see all sides of any story, including my own. As I say, self-centred!

That middle-of-the-road attitude is very Canadian, and also, I was to discover, very Icelandic. I didn't invent it; I detected it. In the early days, the new Western Icelanders comprised about one-tenth of the population of Winnipeg; they must have had some effect. Leaving old hardships to face new ones only confirmed the attitude they brought with them, the one expressed so eloquently in the sagas, that the only thing one has is one's name. Cattle die and kindred die, but the name of a good person lives on. One simply has to endure, that's all. That's enough! It is, too. I find this attitude in Somali taxi drivers and Pakistani clerks and Chinese greengrocers—first-generation Canadians who are proud of having endured and survived, whether it's a Canadian winter or Canadian taxes. Other than this ability to endure, Canadian characteristics are hard to define. Most people do it with negatives: not American, not British, not whatever which makes them self-indulgent, self-involved, and very self-conscious. I qualify on those counts, too. I really must be Canadian.

It seems that everything I like, however, from glaciers and waterfalls, poetry and sagas, hard fish and *vínar terta*, elves and trolls—and have I mentioned Nordic men?—everything seems to stem from my Icelandic background. In fact, I am a fully assimilated Western Icelander, or so I thought. I hadn't even realized how powerfully Iceland had influenced me until I began to write these letters, and to assess what I knew. You won't be surprised to learn, Terry, that I kept a travel diary from my two trips to Iceland.

In each I kept asking myself who I was and what I was doing there. It is in the same questing spirit that I have been writing these letters, trying to put into words feelings I never knew I had.

You are probably familiar with that expression "You can't go home again." It doesn't mean literally, but it is still true. In the case of our ancestors who left Iceland, they simply couldn't afford to. Besides, the weather and volcano reports that filtered through with later arrivals made it clear that there really was nothing for them to go back to. Nothing stays the same, even if you try to stand still. In any case, there was no indication that the "defectors" would have been welcome if they had tried to go back.

In my reading of the history of the Icelandic exodus I have come across intimations that the people the emigrants left behind resented them for deserting the ship, so to speak, and that they envied them for surviving and perhaps even succeeding. At the same time, those who left and fled to an environment that was almost as harsh as it was back home silently fumed that no one in Iceland realized what a hard time they were having, or, worse, seemed to miss them. Those feelings were not unique to Icelanders. Bill's father ran away from his home in Scotland, and was resented for deserting the family and "making good," so it was thought, in Canada. I have heard similar stories from others, no matter where they came from. Some of the worst rancour I have seen is in Winnipeggers who are furious at friends or neighbours who have moved to Vancouver. "How dare they! I'm telling you, they'll miss Manitoba sunshine!" Speaking of which, that's about the only thing the Icelandic immigrants gained, was sunshine. The first winter the settlers spent in New Iceland, the temperature dropped to -47° Fahrenheit. That could make anyone miss lava ash. But no one went back.

It takes the second, third or even fourth generation to be curious about the land of their ancestors, or maybe not. The Western Icelanders I went with to take a look seemed to be only mildly curious. I think some of them were shocked by what they found. Coming from their relative ease in the new world, so hard won by their pioneering parents, they weren't prepared for stony farms and cold fishing villages. Nor did they seem overwhelmed by the beauty of Iceland's natural resources. When I took the boat trip on the melt-water of Vatnajökull, I was one of three of the 60 passengers on our tour bus willing to fork out $20 U.S. for the privilege. Maybe that was too expensive for my fellow-travellers. However, they were also unwilling to pay two dollars for a trip into the past at the Glaumbær Museum, or simply to spend a little energy trudging down the slope to creep behind the water at Seljalandsfoss. They seemed remarkably indifferent to the land that had, if not exactly fostered, at least produced their kinfolk. That still astonishes me. One of my more adventurous bus-mates said snidely that it was because many Icelanders are tight. If that is so, then who can blame us? It may be a trait that has been bred into us over the taut, fraught centuries.

I believe that the very act of ancestral survival of all those hardships has given the Icelandic people a drive and a focus and a sense of identity that has never left them, nor their progeny, even the ones who left for the New World, —and not the act only, but the awareness of it, the record for all to see and learn from. In a way, I suppose Canada continued the education of this northern people, under-lining what they had already learned. You don't get something for nothing. You don't get anything without hard, hard work and deprivation. Often ridiculed as the Puritan work ethic, this attitude, too, is very Icelandic, very Canadian. What you do get is worth every penny, every effort it cost, and it must be appreciated to the hilt. There's no such thing as a free lunch. Enjoy it while you can, it's the secret of survival.

Writer and artist Julia Cameron, in her book *The Artist's Way*,[1] has this to say about survival: "Survival lies in sanity, and sanity lies in paying attention." I think this is how the Icelanders survived, by paying very close attention. Until recently, when I began to examine the statement, I considered this to be a good attitude. Stress management people keep telling us how important it is to live in the present, to cherish the moments, to sniff the flowers on the way by, and it seems to be good advice. What I didn't realize is that if you overdo it, you can lose your past and your future, as well. The past becomes a place you cannot emotionally afford to return to, and you have to forget the future entirely because it's too scary, presenting too many questions for a person intent on today to be able to handle. Suddenly the flower-sniffing becomes an avoidance mechanism and loses its charms.

I thought of social historian Christopher Lasch in his book *The Minimal Self*[2] who refers to the "banality of survival," suggesting that the very act of paying attention to the details at hand can be a wasteful way of hoarding life. Lasch lists other survival strategies that may work for people in desperate extremes, such as "selective apathy, emotional disengagement from others, renunciation of the past and the future (and) a determination to live one day at a time," but surely it's clear that if these tactics are carried on for too long, survivors are in danger of losing their humanity—unless they have a creative outlet, unless they have the edge granted them through self-awareness, unless their stories have been told. "Having been," says psychotherapist Viktor Frankl, "is the surest kind of therapy."[3]

1 Julia Cameron, *The Artist's Way*, New York: Jeremy P. Tarcher/Putnam, a member of Penguin Putnam Inc., 1992.
2 Christopher Lasch, *The Minimal Self: Psychic Survival in Troubled Times*, New York, London: W.W. Norton & Company, 1984.

Frankl, a survivor of a death camp, developed his own theory of survival, which he called *logotherapy*, based on an understanding of an individual's past and a revision of the meaning of existentialism. Terry, I think the Icelanders may have been the first existentialists in the Western World, or, at least, the first recorded ones. They learned early on, the hard way, that to live was to suffer. Frankl suggests that survival depends on finding meaning in suffering. The Icelanders found the meaning of their suffering through the sagas, telling their stories through the centuries, listening, telling, remembering and surviving.

At first, all immigrants, no matter where they come from, must adopt a survival mentality. Icelanders coming to North America had this advantage: they already had a survival mentality, a highly developed one, having survived centuries of deprivation. They also possessed that saving point of difference. Western Icelander Bill Holm, poet, academic and self-proclaimed professional Minneotan,[4] says in the title essay of his book, *The Music of Failure*,[5] that the very act of facing their failures had enabled the Icelanders to survive. They had, in effect, "eaten their own failures." They had accepted them, internalized them, if you will, to the point that they "had no need to be other than [themselves]." Then they "created a literature that held the national ego together through six hundred years of colonial domination, black plague, leprosy, volcanic eruption, and famine that by 1750 reduced this already half-starved population to half the size it had been when it was settled." He's talking about psychic survival, in itself a kind of victory. I think that people who "swallow their failures" have

---

3 *Man's Search for Meaning: An Introduction to Logotherapy,* a revised and enlarged edition of *From Death Camp to Existentialism,* by Victor E. Frankl., tr. Ilse Lasch; preface by Gordon W. Allport. New York: A Touchstone Book, Simon and Schuster, 1962.
4 He lives in Minneota, Minnesota, in a house that cost $5,000 in 1977 and has since steadily declined in value.
5 Bill Holm, *The Music of Failure*, Marshall, MN: Plains Press, 1985.

managed to assert that victory over defeat, in the end, the only kind of victory. They may have swallowed their failures but they weren't driven by them. Instead, they are drawn by the future, by hope, by values long established in the past but ever present and ever aspired to in the future.

Another Western Icelander seems to agree with the idea of the efficacy of failure. Judge and historian Walter J. Lindal, in his book, *The Icelanders in Canada,*[6] claims there is an "Icelandic mind" that enabled the settlers to survive. He adds that this mindset is not a monopoly, that it is achievable by others, combining what they retained from the past with the changes the new environment forces on them. In fact, he says it is one of the most salient characteristics of all immigrants, their drive to survive—no, to thrive—in a new environment. Lindal refers to historian Arnold J. Toynbee's phrase, "the virtues of adversity," which he says wield a stronger influence than mere expedience. I gather Lindal thinks that adversity imposes a tempering process. I am reminded of the saying that "the same flame that melts butter tempers steel." I believe that the character of the Icelanders, like that of many of the emigrants who left Europe during that historic exodus to the New World, had already been forged in adversity. Canada added another degree of pressure—though not heat!

Through common experiences they develop a common psychology, one of endurance. Canadian experience teaches them—us—that if we can stick it out, we've won. We survive and go on in strength.

For survival to have any meaning, it is important always to know who is surviving, that is, who the self is, and then, to take responsibility for that self, whatever it may turn out to be. I guess what I'm saying, Terry, is that when you have a strong sense of self, you can go on from there,

---

6 In the Canada Ethnica II series, Ottawa. Printed by National Publishers Ltd. and Viking Printers, Winnipeg, 1969. No ISBN.

secure in the knowledge that at least no one can take that away from you. We're not talking self-actualization here, one of American psychologist Abraham Maslow's favourite terms, but self-transcendence. And still we rise. So there you are, here I am. Blue and white, fire and ice, story and poetry, all these things that seem so purely Icelandic are also purely me. They are building blocks, components of my self-ness. I don't mean only these specifics, I mean that something like race memory has imprinted a self upon me—and on you, too. I also know that somewhere along the line, I took over and shaped what I have encountered. When you were in school did you have to memorize the poetic passage[7] that goes "I am a part of all that I have met"? I did, and I think of it often because I truly am part of all that I have met, and of what my/our ancestors met before me.

I know that the immigrant experience is much the same for everyone: the wrench, the separation, the struggle, the fear, the loss, the assimilation, also the resentment—on both sides. Isn't it ironic that the least prosperous and (almost) the worst land the immigrants found was in Manitoba? Utah was warmer; Minnesota, while cold, was more fertile than the area around Lake Winnipeg. The chief difference, of course, and the biggest incentive, apart from the free land (offered elsewhere, on the same terms), was the initial autonomy the Western Icelanders were guaranteed in Keewatin, soon to be part of Manitoba (because of them). The newcomers were able to carry on their own government, education, language and customs, which must have been reassuring as they were struggling to learn the ways of a new land, even foreign methods of fishing and farming. Nothing was easy!

Trapped by weather, by illness (that smallpox epidemic) and by lack of access to other people or facilities, the

---

7 From Tennyson's *Ulysses* (1842).

settlers must have felt devastated and abandoned, not to say discouraged. When the railroad line was extended from Winnipeg up to New Iceland, they welcomed it, not immediately realizing that it was the beginning of homogeneity. It put them at risk of losing their distinctiveness, of becoming just another settlement in the vast mix of North America. It didn't happen, not entirely.

And that's odd, Terry, that it didn't happen. At first glance, Western Icelanders seem to be so easily assimilated into a new community. They are not visibly different from their hosts in North America. They are bright and accommodating; they work hard; they get along; they intermarry, eventually. After all that vicious axe-twirling their Viking ancestors indulged in, they are a mild-mannered people like their kin back in the home island, law-abiding, middle-of-the-road people, by their own account—a lot like Canadians, in fact, which is what they are. So why didn't they disappear? How is it that the town of Gimli, population 2,000, swells by some 40 to 50 thousand people every August when family and friends and kin and curiosity-seekers come to eat *skyr,* honour the Maid of the Mountain and toast Iceland? I maintain, always, that it goes back to the stories our ancestors told each other in the dark. They taught themselves who they were; then they carried their selfness with them.

I'm still not sorry that I didn't stay with you and Lorna to experience a Reykjavik new year. I saw the woodpiles being accumulated all over the country in readiness for the event, all of them, you said, set alight on New Year's Eve. Lorna said she will always remember the view of the city from the hill from which you chose to view the fireworks—private explosions of shared joy. I left early, you remember, in order to get back to my own fire at home, a private light I cherish to illuminate my coming year. Perhaps I do this from an ancestral need to huddle. But I saw the newspaper on New Year's Day with a photograph of Reykjavik the night before, holding the dark at bay with a spectacular light show. No wonder it has been chosen as the city of the Millennium! If anyone knows how to keep the dark at bay, the Icelanders do. Me too, but I do it my way.

As a storyteller, I treasure the fact that the light has never died in them or in us, Terry. That's all I want to do: hold up the light, keep the fire going.

—LOVE, B.J.

CANTO FOUR
—LETTER TO W.H. AUDEN

Well, thanks for going with me on my way.
It's been a varied trip, with lots to see.
And as you've noticed, I had lots to say
About my people and my destiny.
I hope that you had an epiphany—
I do not hide it, I will not be coy:
I was pleased to be surprised by joy.

But if you weren't, that's okay, too. I learned
A lot as I researched and wrote my letters.
It's true that I have been much more concerned
With women's lot than you. We are their debtors.
In wisdom and in sense they are pacesetters.
This is where I should quote Hávamál:
Man is naught without the femme fatale.

(Well, words to that effect, I had to fit
The rhyme.) One other thing I have to say
Before I stop—and this is quite legit—
Do not forget I am Canadian, eh?
Remember that and no one goes astray—
Nor I, though influenced by Nordic views,
I still remember where I pay my dues.

You were a tourist seeking recreation.
I had a reason deeper far than yours

You could look with due deliberation,
An analyst who weighs what he explores,
While I was rapt, enthralled with distant shores.
For me it was a heart-rending collision
As I pursued a kind of double vision.

I've done a lot of reading for this book,
And thinking, too, as writers like to do.
There is no stone I want to overlook—
A heavy task, for Iceland has a few.
I'd one or two ideas to pursue
As well as questions that I had to weigh:
Did Iceland make me what I am today?

Did genes or nurture form my view of life?
Where did I come from and where do I go?
Was I destined to be more than wife?
Was I programmed for this long ago?
(Is this a subject for the last canto?)
I guess the moral, whether first or last,
Is to be careful digging up the past.

—BJW

RECIPE INDEX